WATERSIDE
In Yorkshire

Vale of York, North York Moors
and the Yorkshire Coast

Len Markham

COUNTRYSIDE BOOKS
Newbury, Berkshire

First published 1999
© Leonard Markham 1999

All rights reserved. No reproduction
permitted without the prior permission
of the publisher:

COUNTRYSIDE BOOKS
3 Catherine Road
Newbury, Berkshire

ISBN 1 85306 553 6

Designed by Graham Whiteman
Cover illustration by Colin Doggett
Photographs by the author
Maps by Tom Markham

Produced through MRM Associates Ltd., Reading
Printed by Woolnough Bookbinding Ltd., Irthlingborough

Contents

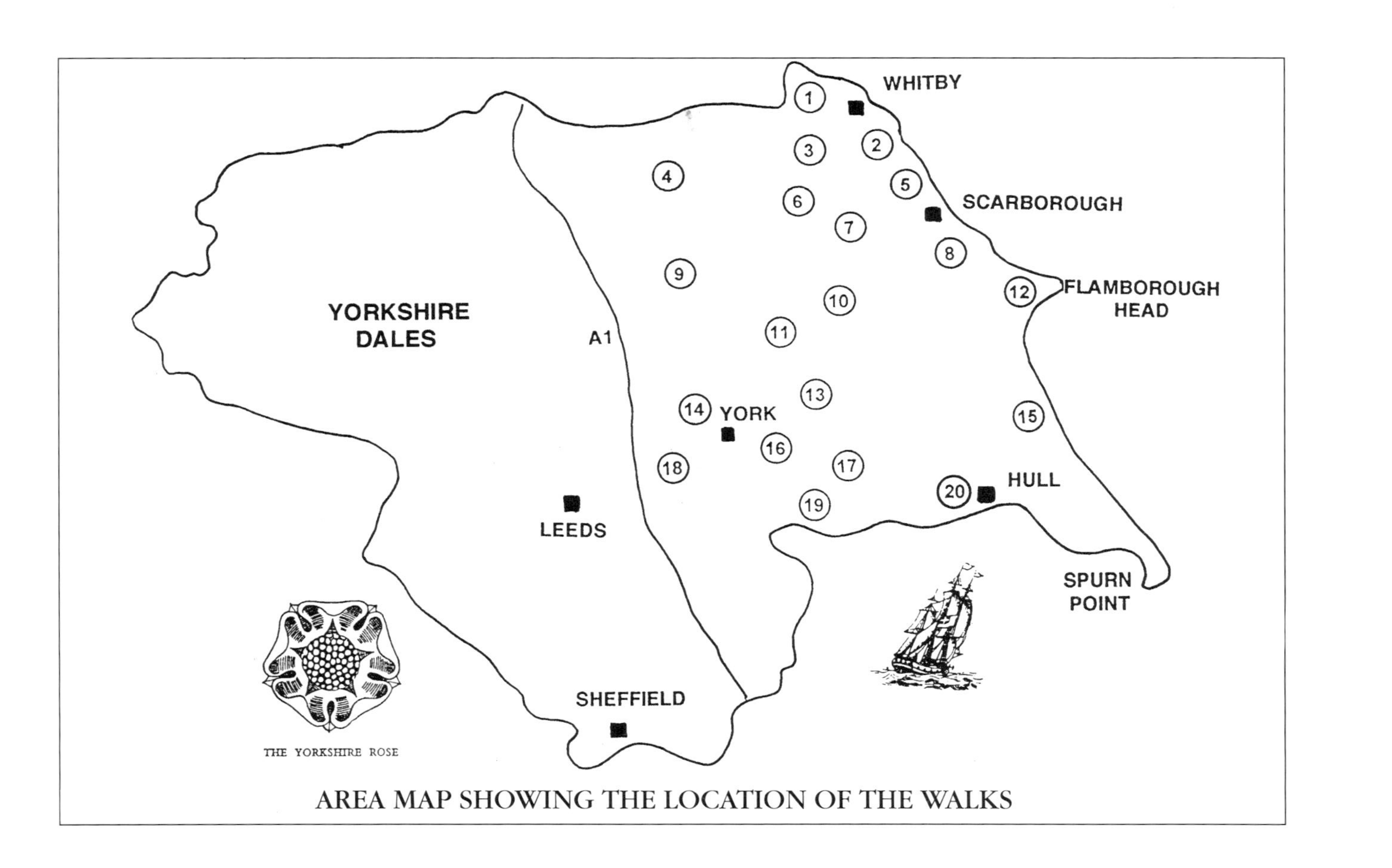

AREA MAP SHOWING THE LOCATION OF THE WALKS

Walk

Publisher's Note

We hope that you obtain considerable enjoyment from this book; great care has been taken in its preparation. Although at the time of publication all routes followed public rights of way or permitted paths, diversion orders can be made and permissions withdrawn.

We cannot of course be held responsible for such diversion orders and any inaccuracies in the text which result from these or any changes to the routes nor any damage which might result from walkers trespassing on private property. We are anxious though that all details covering the walks are kept up to date and would therefore welcome information from readers which would be relevant to future editions.

INTRODUCTION

As a lifelong fisherman, Yorkshire waters have been my constant companions for over 50 years. During that half century I have come to know those waters well, having dipped numerous lines in all the county's major rivers, lakes and ponds as well as in the lesser known streams, becks and canals, not forgetting the depths off the sea coast. I am fascinated by fishing, and beguiled by water in all its manifestations – leaping, bubbling, spray-whipped and still. But such has been my perennial interest in waterside plants, animals and insects that I have missed a thousand bites! No matter, I have enjoyed every minute of my outings, not least the waterside and cliff-top paths that now form the backbone of this book.

Fundamental to life, water has shaped our very existence and it also has a spiritual dimension, enchanting land and seascapes inspiring countless poems and canvases down the years. William Wordsworth watched the sun go down over the mysterious Lake Gormire below Sutton Bank on his wedding day and the artist Turner spent many weeks at his easel capturing the majesty of our rivers. But water can be a backdrop for both the sublime and the deadly. In 1066, the river Derwent at Stamford Bridge witnessed a murderous contest for control of a vital bridge and during the Battle of Towton in 1462, the waters of the Cock Beck ran red with blood. Conflicts at sea were no less sanguinary. In 1779, the fledgling American navy under the command of John Paul Jones fought out a murderous gun duel with English ships in the Battle of Flamborough Head and in more recent times, on 16th December 1914, the German navy bombarded Scarborough causing many injuries and 18 deaths.

Water continues to exert a powerful influence on all our lives and I hope to capture some of its awe and mystery in these waterside walks. Focusing on the great swathe of excellent rambling country generally east of the Great North Road (A1), these walks embrace the green pastures of the Vale of York and the Humber banks, the rolling chalk hills of the Yorkshire Wolds and the rugged valleys, moors and cliff-top villages of the North York Moors. I take great delight in introducing both Yorkshire residents and visitors to some of my favourite rambles, visiting popular beauty spots like Hornsea Mere and not so obvious locations such as Bishop Wilton, the contrasting precincts of York and Goole and the banks of the diminutive river Seven.

As far as practicalities are concerned, none of the walks are too taxing, all being between 2½ and 8½ miles in length. All are within the capacity of both young and old and the only requirements are stout, preferably waterproof, footwear and a kagoule or similar in case it rains.

For the added convenience of walkers, each route is circular and starts from or near a pub or passes one en route. Details of some wayside cafés and teashops are also given, although it should be stressed that all such information is subject to change. Telephone numbers are provided so that you can make advance inquiries about menus and opening times. It is often possible for customers of a pub to leave their cars in the car park while they walk, but the landlord's permission should always be sought first. If you want to park by the roadside, please make sure you consider local residents and be careful not to obstruct any exits and entrances.

Brief details of places of interest within a short driving distance of each walk are included too, to help you plan a full day out if you wish.

Using the simple route descriptions and the sketch maps drawn by my son Tom Markham, all the walks are easy to follow although for further enjoyment the quoted Ordnance Survey Outdoor Leisure or Landranger maps may be used. These are particularly useful for identifying the main features or views.

Finally, may I ask you to follow the Countryside Code, always keeping to the proper paths, closing all gates, keeping dogs on leads and being particularly vigilant about litter. Remember, the best walkers leave only footprints!

The concluding sentence must, however, be reserved for that doyen of all Yorkshire walkers, Alfred J. Brown, who in a 1928 publication railed against the proliferation of cars. His book, all 323 pages of it, is devoted to the adventures of four Yorkshire rivers – the Wharfe, Aire, Ouse and Swale. But let Wharfe speak! 'Let us not forget the high purpose of our Pilgrimage, which is, not only to explore and pay homage to the marvellous beauty of our Fine Shire, without regard to any particular river or any particular Riding: but also to establish once again the Rights of Man, Two-Legged, on the Open Road.'

Len Markham

WALK 1

DALEHOUSE AND STAITHES: SEA LEGGING

After starting gently enough in the quiet hamlet of Dalehouse, our short walk plunges into what was once the workplace of Captain James Cook RN, before we raise the spinnaker in a steep ascent onto the spectacular cliff-top walk known as the Cleveland Way. With spindrift in your nostrils you can race the coasters to the mouldering former iron ore facility at Port Mulgrave before changing tack and heading inland to woodland and the Dales Beck which escorts us back to port.

Staithes

The walk starts in Dalehouse, at the Fox and Hounds, set in a smugglers' nook well away from the prying eyes of the excise men. A bijou inn, it is a treasure not to be found accidentally, the casual visitor naturally gravitating towards Staithes just a short distance to the north. Two small bars with open fires and pew-style seating, reynard's tail for authenticity and an attractive home-cooked menu provide all the incentive you need for jumping ship and leaving the walk for another day. You could linger on the terrace overlooking the quiet lane for hours, contemplating the inscribed stone at your feet "T'was not the beer that put him here. What is there under? This stone was laid for all to see to stand and think and wonder."

The standard choice of meals includes soup of the day, steak and kidney pie, steaks, mixed grill, roast chicken, Yorkshire ham, Cumberland sausage and curry of the day, the daily blackboard list typically offering Burgundy braised beef, fillet steak Rossini, fresh sea trout, sweet and sour pork, crispy roast duck and Whitby cod mornay. The house bitters are Theakston XB, Marston's Pedigree and John Smith's Extra Smooth, complemented by Foster's lager and Guinness and Beamish Red stouts. Opening times are 12 noon to 3 pm and 7 pm to 11 pm (10.30 pm on Sundays). Telephone: 01947 840534.

- **HOW TO GET THERE:** Dalehouse is on a back road near Staithes a few hundred yards south of the A174 Whitby to Middlesbrough road.
- **PARKING:** Park in the pub car park to the rear. Alternatively, use the Pay and Display facilities - well signposted - in Staithes.
- **LENGTH OF THE WALK:** 3½ miles. Map: OS Landranger 94 Whitby or Outdoor Leisure 27 North York Moors - Eastern area (inn GR 778179).

THE WALK

1. Turn left from the inn along the lane up Dalehouse Bank to the main road then turn right along the footway for 100 yards and go left downhill into Staithes.

Recoiling from the waves, wrapped snugly in a cleft of a precipitous beck, the fishing village of Staithes is like one of the ammonite fossils that can be found in the local cliffs. Protected by the girding arms of Cowbar Nab and Penny Steel, it tumbles to the sea in a jumble of narrow alleyways and red roofs, a flotilla of brightly painted cobbles tugging on their mooring ropes at the brink.

Descend left, dropping down and going left down an alleyway to the bridge over the beck. Turn right onto the main street and go left.

Look out for the wonderfully named ginnels - Boathouse Yard, Slippery Hill, Barrass Square and Gun Gutter. The grocery and

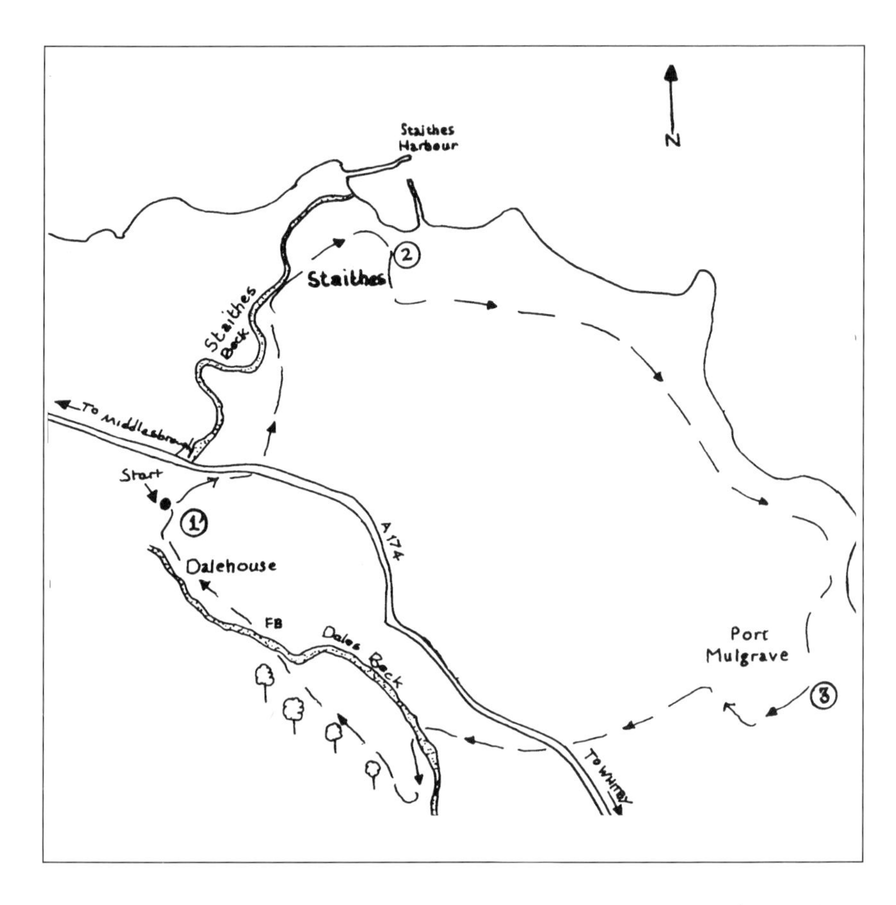

drapery shop where the young James Cook worked in 1740 has long since been washed away but much of the old fabric of Staithes remains enabling visitors to conjure up the scene described just over 100 years ago by John Leyland in his book 'The Yorkshire Coast': 'blue-eyed, ruddy-skinned, picturesque fisher-girls wander along the beach in search of "flithers" for bait, or trip through the narrow alleyways and steep courts of the village with baskets of fish poised upon their heads, while at the doors sit their elders, in the summer-time, knitting, or occupied in the mending of nets'.

Continue to the corner occupied by the Cod and Lobster.

You must call in here for a noggin. I have enjoyed its almost surf-free interior in foul weather and even when the North Sea keeps a discreet distance, it must be one of the most atmospheric inns in England.

2. Turn right opposite the inn up the Church Street bank. Keep ascending and go left, following the Cleveland Way sign to the cliff top. Continue for about a mile to Port Mulgrave.

This inlet was developed for the transhipment of iron ore in the 19th century. Little remains save the blocked up tunnels and the fractured quay which was blown up during the last war to prevent use by the enemy.

3. Turn right along the road towards the former workers' cottages and after 200 yards, go right opposite the telephone box following a public footpath sign down a track. The houses to the right and left belonged to the port managers. Walk on fieldside and swing left on a path, crossing a stile and dropping down fenceside towards the main road. Cross a second stile and continue to the road.

4. Cross the A174 and go right along a lane for 200 yards then go left over a stile, following a public footpath sign into woodland. Drop down left towards the beck, descending wooden steps, swing right and keep descending towards the water swinging left to find a wooden footbridge over it. Cross and go immediately left, following the yellow arrow marker uphill.

5. Go right at the fence, continuing to climb, and after 50 yards swing right, following a yellow arrow marker on a post. Leave the wood and drop down to a stile, going left and right over a bridge, following the beck and the sign to 'Dalehouse'. Turn right on the lane, back to the inn.

Places of Interest Nearby

South-east of Port Mulgrave, the Cleveland Way continues around the edge of *Runswick Bay*, well worth a visit. At Skinningrove, just over the border towards Saltburn (west of Staithes) there is the fascinating *Tom Leonard Mining Museum* (telephone: 01287 642877).

WALK 2

HAWSKER AND ROBIN HOOD'S BAY: A COASTAL TRAMP

To race the coasters along the Cleveland Way to the cliff-perched village of Robin Hood's Bay is to enjoy a truly magical experience but even Merlin on a good day could not create anything like this. With stupendous views, the constant thrashing of the waves and a wind that on occasions gives the un-hatted a free trim, this walk is seriously exhilarating, having the same effect on the complexion as repeated slapping with a salt-soaked cloth. And it will make your heart thump. Not particularly through physical exertion, although there are inclines enough along the way, but rather through the sheer joy of experiencing one of the best routes in England.

The Cleveland Way

The walk begins at the Hare and Hounds inn, in the village of Hawsker just off the Scarborough road. Bright and airy, with open fires in the winter months, this roadside inn has a standard menu offering traditional fare such as steaks, roast chicken and fresh Whitby cod. It is popular for Sunday roasts (booking advisable). The house ales are Theakston and John Smith's bitters and Beamish Black supported by Stella Artois and Foster's lagers. The inn has an entertainment room for children - table tennis, pool and fruit machines. The game of quoits is played nearby. Opening times are 11.30 am to 3 pm and 7 pm to 11 pm from Monday to Saturday. Sunday hours are 12 noon to 3 pm and 7 pm to 10.30 pm. Telephone: 01947 880453.

Robin Hood's Bay has numerous alternative refreshment options and, during the summer months, there is a tea room open in the caravan park at Northcliffe.

- **HOW TO GET THERE:** Hawsker is just 250 yards off the A171 Scarborough to Whitby road, 4 miles from Whitby.
- **PARKING:** Park in the inn car park or on the roadside. Alternatively, Pay and Display car parking is available in Robin Hood's Bay if you want to start the walk from there.
- **LENGTH OF THE WALK:** 6 miles. Map: OS Landranger 94 Whitby or Outdoor Leisure 27 North York Moors - Eastern area (inn GR 927076).

THE WALK

1. Turn left from the inn for 30 yards, cross the road and go straight forward, following the public bridleway sign down a track at the side of a farm. Continue to the old railway bridge, cross and go immediately right over a stile, dropping down steps and swinging right to the former railway track. Turn left and walk on to the junction with a metalled road then go left downhill along a quiet lane towards the sea.

2. Swing right and drop down, crossing the Oakham beck, then go left uphill to the Northcliffe Holiday Park. Turn right in front of the office (tea room to the right) and follow the diversion signs, going left into the caravan parking area, dropping downhill on the access way. In the bottom, go right for 20 yards and left descending to the cliff edge and the Cleveland Way sign.

3. Turn right and continue along the distinctive path to Robin Hood's Bay.

You will pass through the National Trust owned land known as 'Bay Ness'. Interpretation boards point out salient features such as the

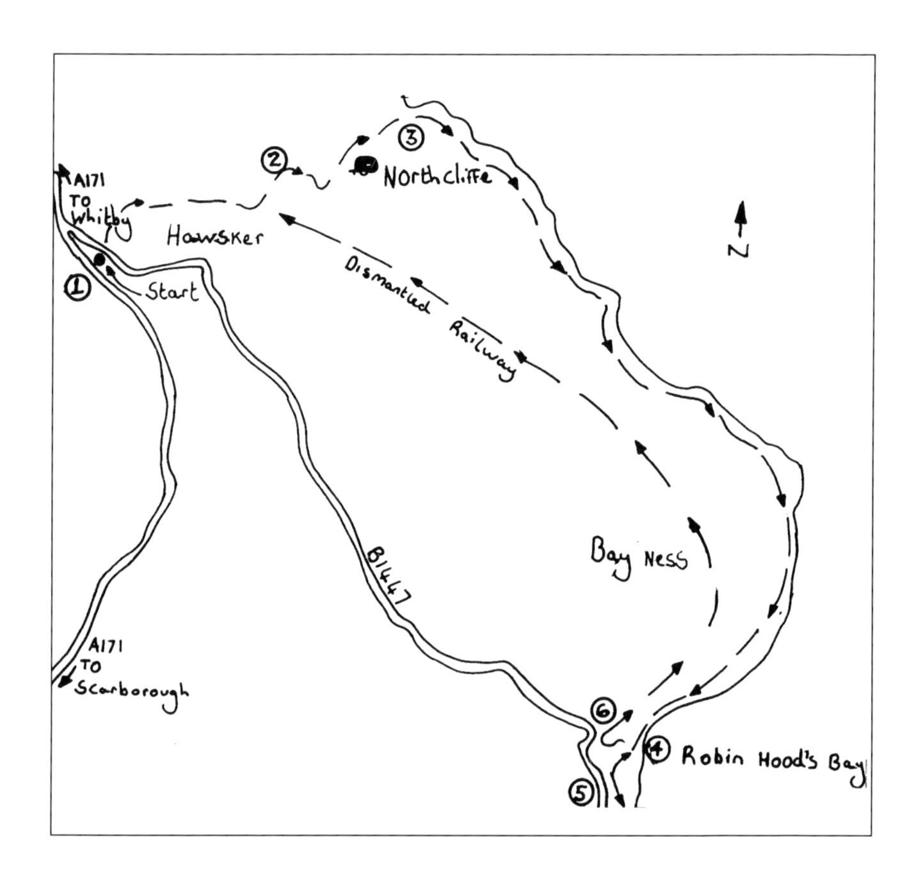

Rocket Post Field. It was planted with a replica mast that was used as a practice target by the coastguard until 1980. Eventually, the grand sweep of Robin Hood's Bay and the cliff at Ravenscar come into view.

4. Leaving the path, continue down Mount Pleasant North and go left at the main road onto the cliff top, descending down the exceptionally steep bank into the village.

Can ***you*** *find your way along Jim Bell's Stile, The Dock, Flagstaff Steps and Tyson's Row? And will you discover the Bay Hotel wherein I had one of my wettest adventures? I quote a description from my book 'Clarty Strands – A Walking Tour of the Yorkshire Coast': 'an inter-tidal hostelry offering impromptu sea-showers whilst contemplating one's dangly bits. I was enthroned until the wave struck and poured through the open window. Curtains, toilet paper*

Cliffs along the Cleveland Way

and ankled trousers did little to absorb the pool and business was adjourned until I found the ladies.'

5. Retrace your steps to the end of Mount Pleasant North and go left, following the 'Railway Path' sign.

6. Turn right through a gate back onto the line of the old railway and continue to the junction with the metalled road that you walked along at the outset. Cross this and walk on to the railway bridge. Go right up the bank and left over the bridge, back to the inn.

Places of Interest Nearby

Besides fossil collecting on local beaches and cliffs and wonderful walks on *Fylingdales Moor* (south of Hawsker) there are the multiple attractions of *Whitby*, among them the *Cook Museum* (telephone: 01947 601900), the *Dracula Experience* (telephone: 01947 601923), *St Mary's church* and the 199 steps up from the harbour, *Whitby Abbey* (ruins), genuine kippers and sea fishing trips.

WALK 3

EGTON BRIDGE: IN PURSUIT OF GOLIATH FRUIT AND GREENGRASS

Using an old toll road, country lanes and footpaths, our splendid circular walk never strays far from a river that is doubly blessed by salmon and that real Yorkshire tyke of a bird, the dipper. The circuit begins at the Postgate Inn. You may find another chirpy tyke, Claude Jeremiah Greengrass of 'Heartbeat' fame, in its chimney corner. The TV series uses the inn - renamed the Black Dog - for filming.

The pub at the start of the walk.

Nicholas Postgate has left an indelible mark on the history of Egton Bridge. A Catholic priest who became a martyr when over 80 years old, he tramped the moors of North Yorkshire spreading the faith for two decades before being executed in 1679. He is remembered in Egton's church dedicated to St Hedda. More prosaically - I think he might have approved - his memory also lives on in the local inn. It is said to be built on the site of his house and it bears his name.

Perversely, it has taken an inspired modernisation to restore the Postgate to its original best with an old Yorkshire range, stone flagging, exposed beams, rustic artefacts and a stuffed pike creating the sort of image that so inspired Hilaire Belloc: 'When you have lost your inns, drown your empty selves, for you will have lost the last of England.' Food is served in the lounge bar and an attractive side restaurant, imagination and tradition combining in dishes such as 'great balls of fire' (deep fried chicken in a jalapeno batter), mushroom and chestnut parcels, steak and ale pie and Whitby cod. The house ales are Theakston, Tetley, Boddingtons and Kilkenny. Lager drinkers can opt for Foster's or Kronenbourg. Guinness is also on draught. Opening times from Monday to Sunday inclusive during the summer months are 11 am to 11 pm (10.30 pm on Sundays). During winter, the shortened hours are 11 am to 3 pm and 7 pm to 11 pm (10.30 pm on Sundays). The inn has five letting bedrooms and a pleasant patio. Telephone: 01947 895241.

- **HOW TO GET THERE:** Egton Bridge is south-west of Whitby, 3 miles south of the A171 Guisborough to Whitby road.
- **PARKING:** Park in the inn car park. Alternatively, free signposted parking is available nearby. Go under the railway bridge, past the church and turn right.
- **LENGTH OF THE WALK:** 3 miles. Map: OS Landranger 94 Whitby or Outdoor Leisure 27 North York Moors – Eastern area (inn GR 805053).

THE WALK

Sitting picturesquely alongside the river Esk, Egton Bridge keeps a luscious secret. Big, bulging, hairy and in shades of green and flushing red, legendary fruits are nurtured here, with the annual Egton Bridge Old Gooseberry Show producing exhibits the size of golf balls. Scenically the best part of Eskdale, Egton Bridge produces some cracking fruit pies and a fair haul of fresh run salmon and although remote and at the foot of a 1 in 3 incline it has its own railway station.

1. Turn right downhill past St Hedda's Primary School (the gooseberry show takes place here each year). Continue past the Catholic church.

The church was built in 1866. On an outside wall are 15 panels showing biblical scenes. In the garden is a grotto remembering the miracle of Lourdes.

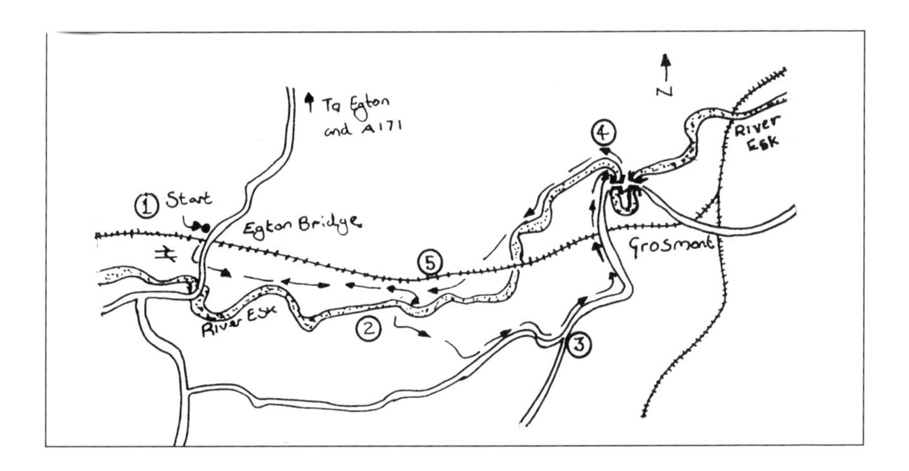

Cross the road and go left, following the footpath sign to Grosmont along the estate track (this was the former toll road). Walk on for about ¾ mile.

2. Turn right, following a public footpath sign at the side of a whitewashed farmhouse. Cross the drive and go through a gate, dropping down over a meadow to a footbridge over the Esk. Cross, bear right and swing left to a footpath sign. Turn left, following the wood edge to a stile. Cross and turn immediately right to find a further stile.Cross into the wood and bear left at an angle uphill, following the line of beech trees until the path becomes more pronounced. Swing right and climb directly forward then go left to a stile. Leave the wood, crossing the stile and turning right uphill over a meadow, walking parallel with the hedge and aiming for the first big tree to the left of the farmhouse. Cross the wall steps and turn left on the quiet lane.

3. At the junction, go left.

A sign reads: 'Deep Ford Ahead - Frequently Impassable'. The Esk is prone to flooding. In 1930, after heavy rains, the swollen river caused extensive damage along its length and Egton Bridge lost most of its crossing which had survived since 1758. But the booted need not worry! The waters may rage. There is a stout footbridge to keep us dry shod.

Drop steeply down, cross the railway bridge and swing right, walking over the footbridge to the far bank of the river. Go left on the road for 100 yards.

4. Go left along the estate road, signposted to 'Egton Bridge 1 mile'. Walk on to the fishing sign.

To your left, steps have been cut into the bank and a guiding wire fixed to the trees to enable fishermen to descend to a favourite salmon pool. In the bottom is a brick-built shelter and belvedere.

Continue along the road to the Toll House (note the old toll charges on a board affixed to the house wall).

5. Retrace your steps back to the inn.

PLACES OF INTEREST NEARBY

Grosmont is the terminus of the North Yorkshire Moors steam railway - see walk 7 (telephone: 01751 472508). *Goathland* (to the south) can be reached by steam train, between spring and autumn, and is the setting for 'Heartbeat'. At *Glaisdale* (west of Egton Bridge) you can see the romantic Beggars Bridge. Then there are the many attractions of *Whitby* (see walk 2).

WALK 4

HUTTON RUDBY: A LEVEN TREAD

A sizeable tributary of the Tees, the river Leven drains the northern flanks of the Cleveland Hills. Serpentine and reclusive, this most enigmatic of Yorkshire rivers flows through a landscape that gave Lewis Carroll his inspiration and to seek it out is to catch just a glimpse of the Sockburn Worm, that fearsome dragon that once terrorised the neighbourhood just seven miles to the west. Our route follows the Leven valley west to the outskirts of Crathorne and then accompanies the stream north on a delightful woodland path. Like the white rabbit, the Leven affords us only fleeting views but, on returning to Rudby, we will be as intimate as any rambler can be with a river without falling in.

The Bay Horse at Hutton Rudby.

Hutton Rudby is really a cluster of three villages that collectively were satirised in the ancient Cleveland folk rhyme:

'Hutton, Rudby, Enterpen –
Far more rogues than honest men.'

Like Buda and Pest, the settlement is separated by a river, the Leven carving a deep glen spanned by a fine arched bridge built in 1755. At the heart of the village is a spacious tapering green with appetising views of the distant hills. And what a heart! Any village that cares for its green, war memorial and old water pump like this has a really big one. The carefully cut sward is a fine place for loafing but there is something in the unseen murmur of the river and the beckoning views that sets the blood tingling in the phalanges region. So you will want to lace up quickly, perhaps choosing the finest place for knot tying I have come across in many a walk. If there were rosettes for pub gardens, the blooming Bay Horse on North Side would win hands down. Its flower filled garden overlooking the valley is very popular for barbecues on summer evenings. Internally, the low beamed pub is deceptively spacious with a number of dining options, having a bar, lounge and restaurant all tastefully decorated.

The extensive, constantly changing menu gives the widest cosmopolitan choice, a wide range of starters such as carrot and coriander soup and green-lipped mussels heading blackboard listings which may include loin of pork, roast leg of lamb, steak and mushroom pie, confit of duck with blackcurrants, grilled lemon sole, whole lobster and pan fried salmon. A real ale inn, the Bay Horse offers Nick Stafford's Stud - brewed locally at the Hambleton Brewery near Thirsk - Black Sheep, Boddingtons, Whitbread Trophy Special and Castle Eden bitters, various lagers and Murphy's Irish stout. Opening times from Monday to Saturday are 12 noon to 3 pm and 6.30 pm to 11 pm. Sunday hours are 12 noon to 3 pm and 7 pm to 10.30 pm. Telephone: 01642 700252.

- **HOW TO GET THERE:** About 6 miles south of Middlesbrough, Hutton Rudby is easily accessible off the A19, going through Crathorne. Visitors from the south can travel along the A19 and the A172, going second left along the by-road signposted to Potto.
- **PARKING:** Park in the pub car park. Alternatively, extensive parking is available round the village green.
- **LENGTH OF THE WALK:** 6 miles. Map: OS Landranger 93 Middlesbrough and Darlington area or Outdoor Leisure 26 North York Moors–Western area (inn GR 471064).

THE WALK

1. Turn right from the pub along North Side, following the edge of the village green, and walk uphill. Turn right again by Eva's Cottage, following the public footpath sign. Swing right down steps and continue over a stile, walking on the riverside to the bridge. Go through a gate and turn left across the Leven bridge.

You are now in the parish of Rudby where All Saints' church is picturesquely situated. It is worth visiting for its colourful hassocks alone. Pevsner describes the Elizabethan pulpit as 'a precious piece'.

2. Go hard left on the right bank of the Leven over the church car park and walk down the un-named lane (not South View) for about 200 yards and find a stile on the right by a wrought iron gate. Cross right and continue uphill on a water authority concrete access road, swinging left downhill to the sewage works. Go left by the works entrance and right along the river bank, swinging right over a stile. Cross a second stile and walk on fieldside, arcing right to the corner of the field. Swing left for 25 yards, then, where the track forks, go right uphill into woodland. At the edge of the wood, go left along its perimeter to a lane.

3. Turn left by the bungalow known as Blue Barn along a wide track and continue along this track for about a mile to a gate near a farmstead.

4. Cross a stile, turning right downhill on a track to a second gate. Go through, swinging right by the Mill House. Swing left on the lane towards the Leven river bridge and go right on the lane, following the signpost to High Foxton Farm. Walk on uphill and, at the bend, arc left to the corner of a wood, crossing a small footbridge to a gate. Go through and follow the distinctive woodland track above the river. At the cottage, turn left and cross a stile, aiming diagonally right for a gate in the field corner. Go through and continue along the woodland edge, following the yellow arrow marker downhill to a footbridge over a ravine. Walk up to a stile. Cross and go left, following a yellow arrow marker heading towards farm buildings over a meadow on a track.

5. Turn sharp right on a farm track.

The conical shape of Roseberry Topping comes into view on the left. The Cleveland Hills panorama unfolds in front.

At the junction with the lane, turn left past the pond and walk on for about 500 yards, going right through a gate hedgeside along a track (no sign).

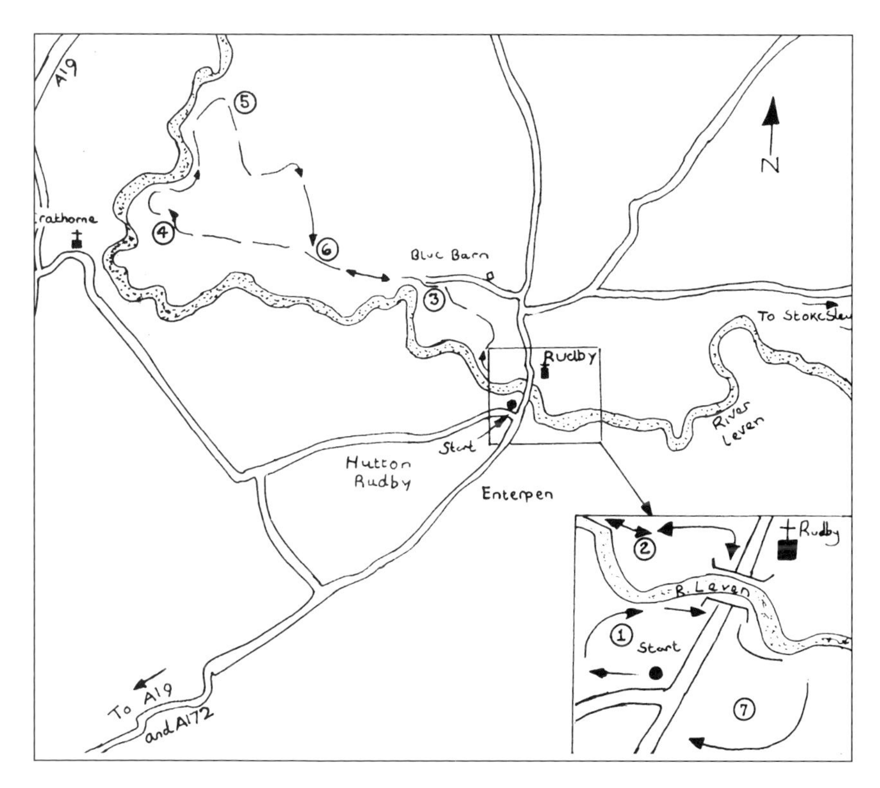

6. At the next intersection of tracks, turn left, retracing your steps back to the church. Cross the bridge right and go sharp left, following the public footpath sign down the slope to the river bank. Turn right.

7. Continue upstream along the bank.Cross two stiles and walk on to a kissing gate and a third stile. Cross and turn right on a back lane, walking uphill past the Hutton Rudby sign. Turn right at the road and continue to the pub.

Places of Interest Nearby

Captain Cook's Schoolroom Museum in Great Ayton, north-east of Hutton Rudby (telephone: 01642 722030). *Ormesby Hall* near Middlesbrough, with its 5 acre garden (telephone: 01642 324188). *Mount Grace Priory* (NT), off the A19 near Osmotherley (telephone: 01609 883494). *Roseberry Topping*, a miniature Matterhorn, is a couple of miles beyond Great Ayton.

WALK 5

CLOUGHTON AND HAYBURN WYKE: A SEASIDE SCRAMBLE

The invigorating and ruggedly picturesque Yorkshire coast has the pull of a spring tide. Take a draught of salt air and catch just a glimpse of the sea from Cloughton and we will have you prancing like the Skegness sailor. The spectacular heritage coast hereabouts is traversed by the Cleveland Way. Our expedition begins quietly by the Cloughton Beck, then follows this famous cliff-top path to Hayburn Wyke where a waterfall tumbles onto the beach. Hayburn Wyke - the term wyke or wick is Norse for a small creek or bay - is fringed by a dense grove of emerald trees, a brawling beck throwing itself impetuously between the boughs and a tumble of great boulders, ferns and flowers sprouting from every crevice. When we can tear ourselves away from this immensely beautiful spot, we return to Cloughton on a former railway track, now a delightful footpath.

Hayburn Wyke

Our walk begins at the dapper Red Lion inn in Cloughton, a winding village that straddles the main Scarborough to Whitby road. Decorated with black and white photographs of local views, with a traditional, homely bar and a snug, both warmed by open fires in winter, the Red Lion is a convenient staging post for the Cleveland Way, having four letting bedrooms. While sea views beckon, you can choose from a menu that includes soups, mixed grill, roast chicken, gammon and egg, fried haddock and steak pie plus specials. The liquid choices are Camerons, Banks's, including Banks's seasonal guest bitters such as Passion, Fine Fettle and Halcyon Days, Kronenbourg and Foster's lagers and draught Guinness. Opening times from Monday to Saturday are 12 noon to 4 pm and 7 pm to 11 pm (check times in winter). Sunday hours are 12 noon to 10.30 pm. Telephone: 01723 870702.

- **HOW TO GET THERE:** Cloughton is 4 miles north-west of Scarborough on the A171 Scarborough to Whitby road.
- **PARKING:** Park in the inn car park to the rear. Alternatively, park off the sharp A171 bend on the minor road at the northern end of the village.
- **LENGTH OF THE WALK:** 6 miles. Map: OS Landranger 101 Scarborough and Bridlington area or Outdoor Leisure 27 North York Moors – Eastern area (inn GR 000947).

THE WALK

1. Turn right from the inn along the main street and go right after passing the house numbered 20, down an alley. Continue on a footpath to a small bridge over the Cloughton Beck. Cross and go left over the cricket field, following the beck down to a footbridge. Cross left and go right over the lane and a ford, turning left, again following the beck. Continue alongside the football pitch, turning left at the corner on a track to the A171 road.

2. Cross the road and go slightly left down Station Lane, turning left opposite the old railway station along the former railway track. Continue to a bridge and go left up the embankment onto the bridge, turning sharp left onto a lane heading seaward to Cloughton Wyke.

On the left is a crumbling lime kiln and to the right are stirring views of Scarborough Castle.

3. Walk on to the cliffs and go left at the bench, along the path. Continue along the well-defined winding and often precipitous path for about 1½ miles until Hayburn Wyke comes into view. The

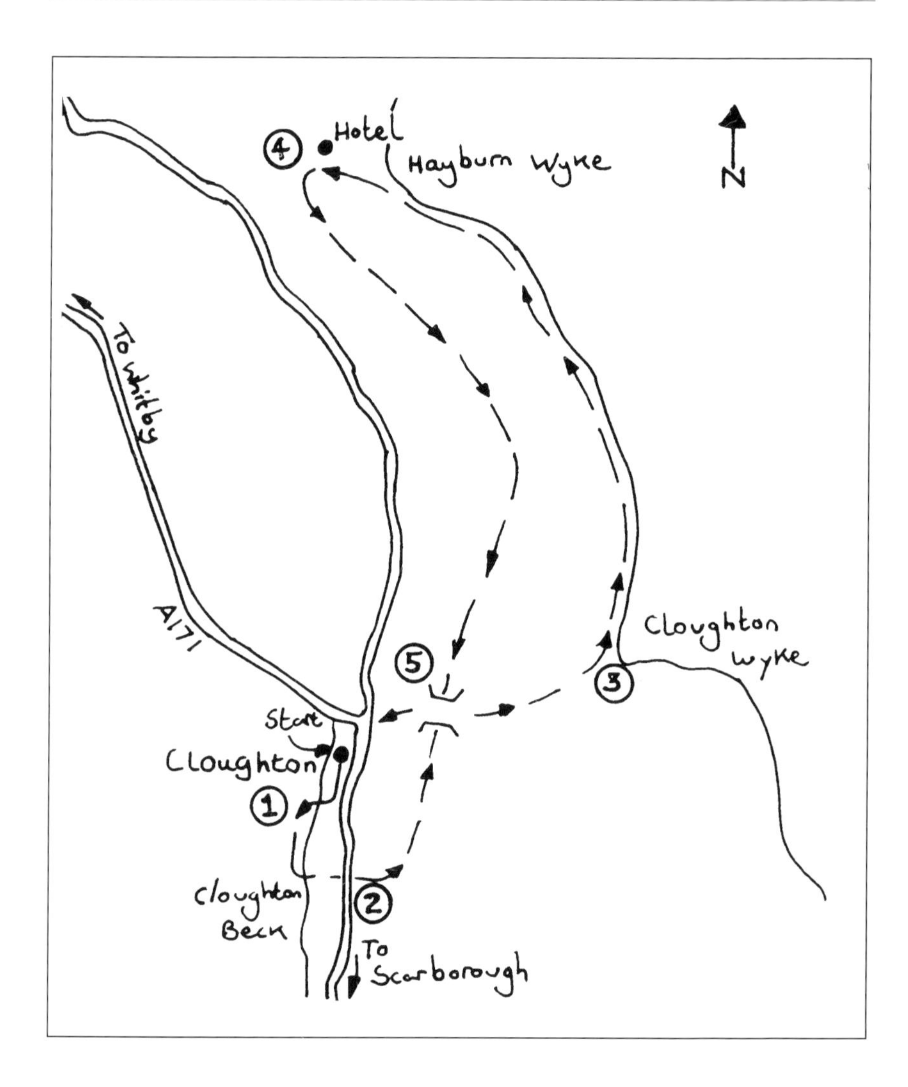

panoramas from the 200 foot cliffs are stupendous.

In Victorian times, special rail excursions from York and Scarborough brought hundreds of visitors to Hayburn Wyke. They rambled in the glen and took tea at the nearby hotel. Today, the railway track is a footpath and the crowds have gone, leaving one of the finest wild places in Yorkshire unmolested. The route down to the beach is difficult especially after wet weather but the struggle to find the cascade that inspired that well known Whitby photographer

Frank Meadow Sutcliffe is well worth the effort. The careful observer may find fossil ferns and mosses in the cliff face. Hayburn Wyke once held a dark secret. In this cove in December 1914, two German battle cruisers hid before they shelled Scarborough and Whitby, killing and wounding nearly a hundred people.

Cross a stile into the dell, going downhill left. Turn right, dropping steeply downhill on a path to the waterfall. Retrace your steps uphill and swing right crossing a stile into a meadow. Steer right and cross a second stile, going right to the Hayburn Wyke Hotel.

4. Turn left on the lane and go left along the railway track continuing for about 1¼ miles to the bridge.

5. Turn right up the embankment and go right again along the lane.

Opposite the Court Green cottages, enjoy a poem on a board: 'a garden is a lovesome thing. . .'

Walk on to the junction and turn left, back to the inn.

Places of Interest Nearby

Scarborough with its many attractions (see walk 8) is only 4 miles away. Forest walks in *Broxa* and *Wykeham* (south-west of Cloughton) are highly recommended, as is trout fishing on the *Scalby Beck*. Northwards up the coast are magnificent *Ravenscar* and *Robin Hood's Bay* (coastal walks, beach exploration and the history of the alum industry). Staintondale (north) has a *Heavy Horse Centre* (telephone: 01723 870458) and to find out about *llama tours along the Cleveland Way* telephone Scarborough Tourist Information office (01723 373333).

WALK 6

ROSEDALE ABBEY: A PRANCE DOWN THE SEVEN VALE

At an arm's length distance, we will follow the Seven down her vale, prising ourselves from her siren gurgles to visit the ancient village of Lastingham with its timeworn and now lamentably dry holy wells. But fret not. We can be fortified at the Blacksmith's Arms by some venerated modern liquid and will return over the lonely Spaunton Moor, before clambering down to the inn. With spectacular long distance views of the National Park this is a blithesome if somewhat taxing walk. Because of the altitude and featureless terrain of the moorland stretch, it is best reserved for fine days.

The popular hotel at the foot of Rosedale Chimney Bank.

Rosedale Abbey takes part of its name from a 12th-century Cistercian nunnery. Save for a fragment of a turret stair, little remains, its stones having been robbed for local buildings after the Dissolution. The secular history of the village is more visible, remnant 19th-century ironstone kilns surviving near the top of the hill.

Within a spark's fly of the old workings, near the foot of the bank, is the commodious, well-appointed and immensely popular White Horse Farm Hotel. Licensed since 1702 it was originally a hostel for miners, two of whom are said to haunt the bars. Under the eye of a menagerie of sporting trophies dominated by the skull of a huge Asian water buffalo, you can choose from a varied selection of seasonal dishes, typically including deep fried Brie with mango mayonnaise, Yorkshire rarebit, mushroom quiche, supreme of chicken, bangers and mash, Barnsley chop, braised rabbit and pheasant and Whitby haddock. The real ale tally is Tetley, Black Sheep and John Smith's bitters backed up with Foster's and Kronenbourg lagers. Customers with real thirsts can opt for four-pint pitchers. The fashionable and intimate restaurant serves a good selection of fine wines and more formal meals. The hotel is open all year and has 15 letting bedrooms. Bar opening times from Monday to Friday are 11.30 am to 2.30 pm and 6.30 pm to 11 pm. Saturday opening is 11 am to 11 pm. Sunday hours are 12 noon to 3 pm and 6.30 pm to 10.30 pm. Telephone: 01751 417239.

- **HOW TO GET THERE:** Rosedale Abbey is about 10 miles north-west of Pickering and is reached via Wrelton (A170) and Cropton. An alternative approach, if you are confident in your brakes, is to go through Hutton-le-Hole, proceeding over Spaunton Moor to the motoring equivalent of a sky-dive.
- **PARKING:** Park in the hotel car park. Alternatively, there is space in the village.
- **LENGTH OF THE WALK:** 8 miles. Maps: OS Landranger 94 Whitby or 100 Malton and Pickering or Outdoor Leisure 26 North York Moors-Western area (hotel GR 725955).

THE WALK

1. Turn right from the hotel over the car park and proceed on a farm track which runs above and parallel with the Seven.

Pass the last of the cottages (Wood Lea) and continue past the pottery shop, swinging right uphill in front of a farmhouse and following a bridleway sign onto the edge of the moor. Go left alongside a wall, keeping forward at the foot of the moor, gradually dropping down nearer the river. You will eventually come to a plaque marking the site of an Elizabethan glassworks.

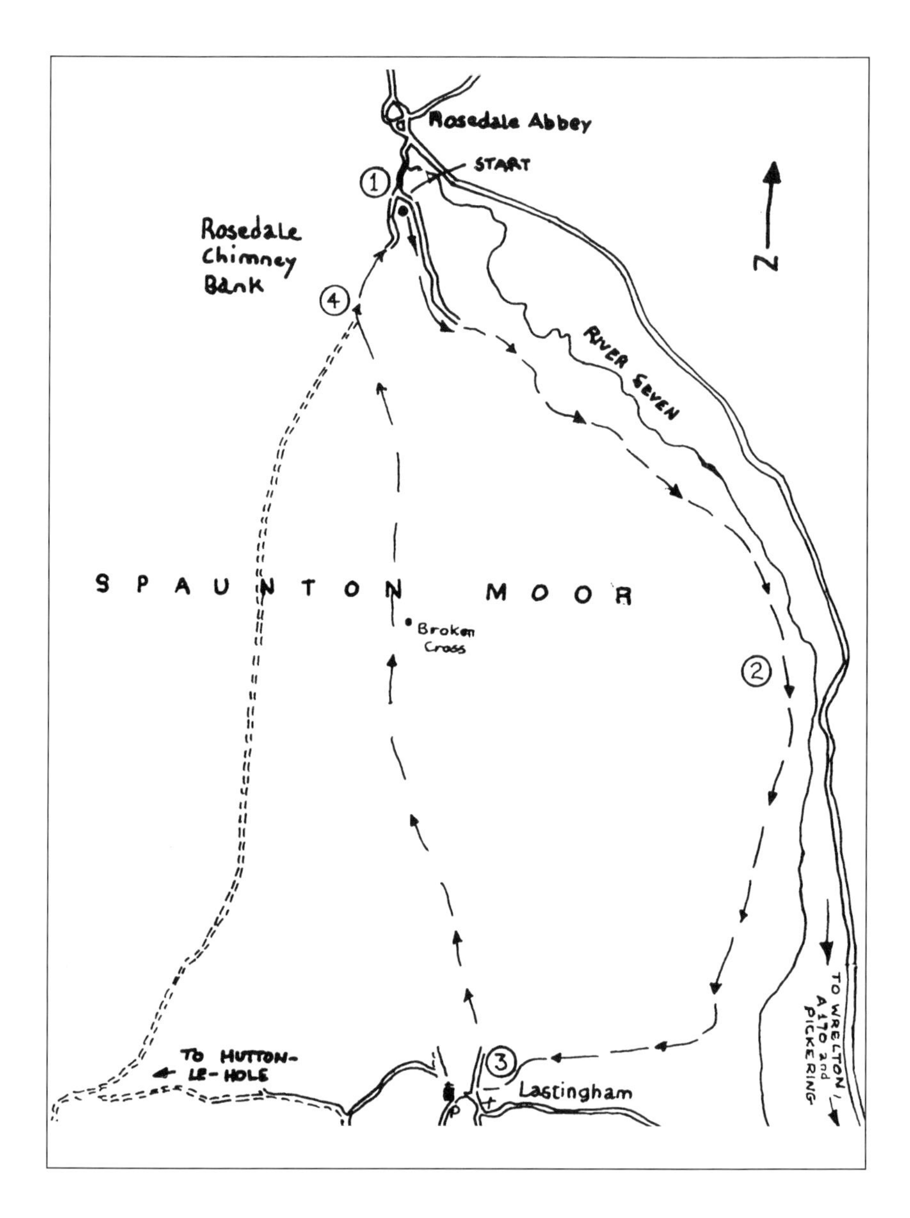

2. Keep going straight forward on a rough track, steering to the right of a farmstead, and go through a gate, swinging right and left on the farm access track for about 300 yards. Go right, following the moorland path, arcing left and walking down wallside to a stile. Cross and steer right between hawthorn trees to go over a beck in the bottom on stepping-stones. Veer left up to a stile. Cross into a new plantation and turn right to a stile. From here follow the distinctive yellow arrow markers over seven fields. In the eighth field, veer left, heading for a stile in the field corner. Cross right and continue down a path along the 'green tunnel', crossing a stile left down several steps into Lastingham.

Left at the junction is one of the sacred wells sought out by pilgrims in centuries past. Right, hard by the Hole Beck, is another. Just up the road is the Blacksmith's Arms in the shadow of the exquisite church of St Mary with its wonderfully atmospheric 11th-century crypt. A monastery was founded here in the year AD 654 by St Cedd and the local wells are dedicated to his memory.

3. Turn right on the lane.

A third well - the best preserved - is on the right opposite Ivy Cottage.

Go through a gate onto Spaunton Moor. Follow the sign to 'Rosedale' on a track to the left. Keep on this track for about 1½ miles then take the left-hand fork (due north compass bearing) coming to a broken cross. Veer left to the road at the summit of Rosedale Chimney Bank.

4. Turn right using the tracks on the broad verge.

To the left are the arches of the ironstone mine kilns.

Continue descending and turn right to the hotel.

Places of Interest Nearby
Ryedale Folk Museum in Hutton-le-Hole: '13 historic buildings show the lives of ordinary folk from earliest times to the present day' (telephone: 01751 417367). *Kirkdale*, off the A170 west of Kirkbymoorside, has a minster (see the famous sundial) and a cave which has yielded tons of prehistoric bones.

WALK 7

LEVISHAM: A PICKERING BECK PLUNGE

In the absence of drogue chutes, good brakes and shock resistant knees are essential requirements for this short but breathtaking walk in the national park. The scents of heather, gorse and pine intermingled with the vapours from passing steam trains combine with stupendous views of Newton Dale and the tinkling of Pickering Beck to make this one of my favourite walks. Our route leaps headlong off the moor to cross a railway line and a hidden ford. It then follows a forest road, accompanying the shy and reclusive beck to Levisham Station before climbing, once again, to the dizzy moor.

The North Yorkshire Moors Railway.

With cliffs up to 200 feet in height, the glaciated valley of the Pickering Beck can be described as a Grand Canyon with chlorophyll, the sweeping multi-green vistas taking in wild moorland pastures and great forests of fir. Study the panoramas from the lofty Skelton Tower and you have an OS map in a perfection of hue and scale, the snaking line in its centre being the route of perhaps the most romantic preserved steam railway in Britain.

Accessed via two 1 in 5 gradients through neighbouring Lockton, the village of Levisham girds itself against the windy moorland arrows like an old time wagon train, offering welcome refreshment in one of the highest inns in the county. Dating back to the 16th century, the Horseshoe Inn has been variously used as a blacksmith's, a tea room, a boarding house and a pub. Its recent refurbishment preserves both character and atmosphere and a splendid fireplace, the rows of muddy but neatly discarded boots in the porch giving as much endorsement as a galaxy of Michelin stars. From the lofty picnic area at the front of the inn, diners can see for miles. This bed and breakfast inn serves a wide range of quality bar meals including steak and kidney pie, Stilton steak, rogan josh, pork dijon, chicken chasseur, Ryedale trout, fresh Whitby haddock and prawn thermidor. The standard menu is complemented by a daily specials board which features game in season. John Smith's bitter, Theakston XB and Old Peculier, Beamish stout and Foster's lager are the bar top offerings. The inn is open Monday to Saturday from 10.30 am to 3 pm and 7 pm (6 pm in summer) to 11 pm. Sunday hours are 12 noon to 3 pm and 7 pm to 10.30 pm. Closed all day Monday in winter. Telephone: 01751 460240.

- **HOW TO GET THERE:** Levisham is about 7 miles north-east of Pickering, off the A169 Pickering to Whitby road. Turn off westwards through the village of Lockton.

  Note: Be careful in icy conditions and make sure your car has been well serviced before you set off.
- **PARKING:** The Horseshoe has a large car park/camping field to the rear. Alternatively, you can park in the village.
- **LENGTH OF THE WALK:** 4½ miles. Map: OS Landranger 94 Whitby, 100 Malton and Pickering or Outdoor Leisure 27 North York Moors – Eastern area (inn GR 833907).

THE WALK

1. Turn right from the inn along the lane signposted to 'Levisham Station'. At the bend, leave the lane and keep going straight forward on a track continuing to a gate. Go through and veer left over the moorland, following the bridleway sign wallside. At the marker post, go left over the moor towards the distant forest (ignore the track that

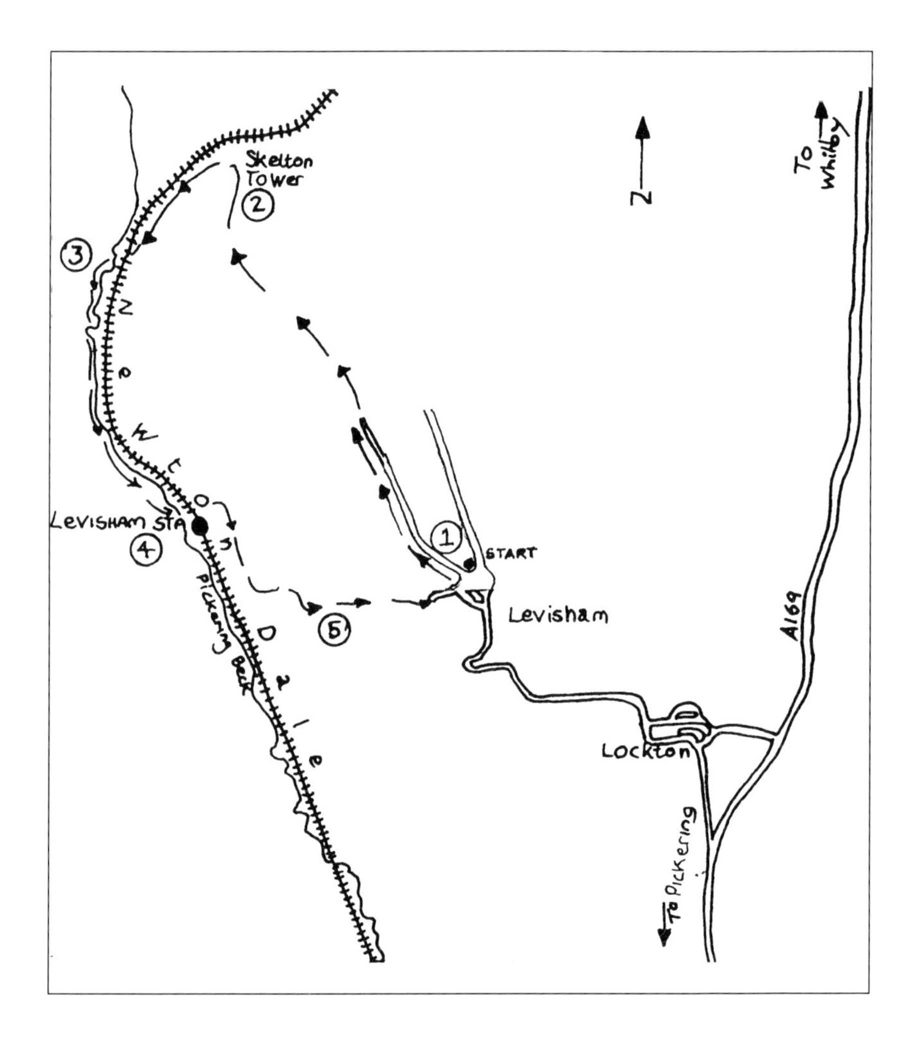

follows the wall sharp left). At the crest, go right, dropping down on a rough track towards the distinctive Skelton Tower. Walk on to the tower.

2. Find the step path below the tower, going left and right and drop off the plateau, going down steeply. At the bottom swing left above the railway and follow the path left then right downhill (route for horses) to a gate at the side of the railway. Go through and cross the line with care, going left for about 40 yards.

3. Turn right off the embankment and drop down to the Pickering Beck, crossing using the stepping stones. Climb up on the far side onto the forest road and go left alongside the beck. Walk on for about 1 mile to Levisham Station.

George Stephenson's Whitby to Pickering Railway was opened on 26 May 1836. After successfully operating for 130 years, the line was closed in the 1960s. It was reopened in May 1973 and is now the country's second longest preserved railway.

Running for 18 glorious miles from Pickering to Grosmont with intermediate stations at Levisham and Goathland (additional dropping off point at Newton Dale Halt) the North Yorkshire Moors Railway is open between spring and autumn. A popular short walk from its second station leads to Levisham village and the Horseshoe Inn.

4. Swing left towards the station and cross the line, using the level crossing. After 100 yards, go right, leaving the road and following a public footpath sign through a gate uphill through a wood. Swing left and leave the wood through a gate, following a yellow arrow marker right across a meadow to a gate and a four directions sign. Go through and follow the signposted route right to the 'Village'.

If there was a British Standard for walking paths this would be it. A green carpet unrolled straight from Olympus, it would have Pan himself dancing.

5. Walk uphill and follow the crest path left and right between cushions of gorse, continuing to a stile. Cross and go left wallside to a second stile. Cross and continue on the lane left into the village, back to the inn.

Places of Interest nearby

In Pickering you will find the *Castle* (ruins) and the charming *Beck Isle Museum* (telephone: 01751 473653). The *North Yorkshire Moors Railway* runs seasonal steam trains along its spectacular 'Heartbeat' route, starting at Pickering (telephone: 01751 472508).

WALK 8

OSGODBY: BAY TRIPPER

This two for the price of one walk takes you to twin bays - Cornelian and Cayton - the lack of vehicular access having preserved their simple charms. Cornelian is the more rugged of the twins, taking its name from the semi-precious, light red or flesh coloured stones that can sometimes be found on the beach. Around Osgodby Point is the more gentle Cayton Bay, its golden sand and green fringes giving more than a soupçon impression of the Riviera.

Cayton Bay

Seascapes that inspired the artist Turner, woods, thickets, reefs, rock-pools, pebbled treasure that had my pockets bulging and two deserted bays with sand the colour of honey and Belgian chocolate. How can nearby Scarborough compete with all this?

Until 1928 Osgodby was just a hamlet. In that year the biggest local landowner put her Old Farm estate up for sale, most of the land going for housing with two former farmhouses becoming a public house. The original barn, after a modern conversion, has now become the Poacher's Pocket. My, how the interior designers have enjoyed themselves! Retaining the original Yorkshire range they have indulged in a rustic spree using stone flags, thatch and cartloads of old farming implements, the country theme extending to a handsomely pocketed cardboard menu in the shape of a greatcoat. Lift the flaps and read the whimsical descriptions of meat and vegetable pie, beef in ale casserole, liver and Yorkshire pudding, baked salmon, ranges of steaks and baguettes and fish and chips. Or choose from the 'Big Screen Specials' - Gone With The Wind (spiced beef curry), Chorus Line (salsa chicken legs) or Emmanuel III (beef and ale in a Yorkshire pudding pool floating with dumplings). The house ales are Camerons Creamy Strongarm Smooth and Banks's Bitter. The lager alternatives are Harp, Foster's and Kronenbourg. Guinness is also available on draught. The opening hours on Monday to Saturday are 11.30 am to 11 pm. Sunday opening is 12 noon to 10.30 pm. Telephone: 01723 584372.

- **HOW TO GET THERE:** Osgodby is south of Scarborough, between the resort and Filey, off the A165. Another approach is via the back road from the A1039 through Folkton and Cayton villages.
- **PARKING:** Park in the pub car park or on the nearby side streets.
- **LENGTH OF THE WALK:** 4½ miles (some steep ascents and descents are necessary). Map: OS Landranger 101 Scarborough and Bridlington area (inn GR 055847).

Note: A feature of this route is the opportunity to explore the numerous rock pools and the strand line. Obviously these are covered at high tide. Therefore, to obtain the maximum enjoyment from the walk, it is best to consult local tide tables before departure (available from local shops).

THE WALK

1. Turn left from the inn alongside the car park edge, following the public footpath sign and walk along the path fieldside. Swing right across a track and go through a gate, continuing on the path at the back of the bungalows. Walk on to Filey Road, the A165. Cross the road and follow the footpath straight ahead, signposted to the beach. (If the diversion is in force, go right following the signs at the side of the bungalow numbered 59 and continue into the residential estate down Osgodby Crescent. Turn left down Osgodby Way to Filey Road. Turn left for 150 yards and go right across the road to the footpath sign to the beach.

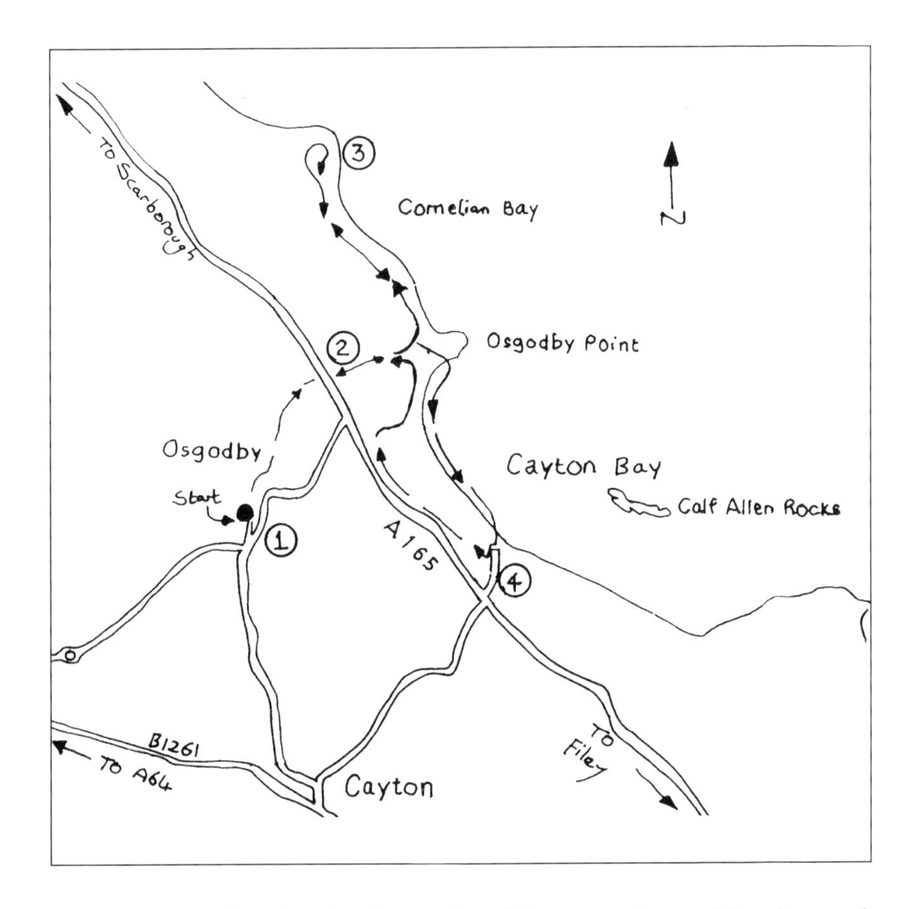

2. Walk on to the Cleveland Way sign. There are views of Scarborough and its castle to the left. Turn left along the cliff path for about ¼ of a mile, veering right down steps into a wood. Drop down and rise up again on a winding path. Leave the wood to rejoin the coast path, continuing to the turning circle. Turn right onto the headland and take the left-hand path, dropping downhill. Swing right on the rough track to Cornelian Bay.

The rocky ledge on the left is good for fishing. Lapidarists head right. For hundreds of years visitors searched amongst the shingle for cornelian, jasper and agate. Prospectors like me are now a rarified breed and you can sift through the cache of stones with little company, taking home some of the wonderfully multi-hued and textured gems for your fish tank. Look out for the delicious looking chocolate sand. It looks appetising enough to sprinkle on your ice-cream!

3. Return up the rough track but instead of going left, keep on the track, arcing left to the turning circle. Return on the outward route to the Cleveland Way sign. Go left downhill into a National Trust wood, steering left at the fork. Continue the descent to Cayton Bay. Walk along the strand past the Second World War pill boxes to the sea wall and turn right up the concrete steps, swinging left up the cobbled access road for about 150 yards.

4. Turn right over a stile, following the Cleveland Way sign. Follow the yellow arrow marker to a second stile. Cross and continue to a third stile, crossing left to the A165. Turn right along the footway for about 600 yards into Osgodby. Turn right at the National Trust sign into woodland down steps. At the intersection of paths (acorn sign) go left and turn left again (acorn sign) at the next intersection. Keep left, going uphill to the Cleveland Way sign. Retrace your steps back to the inn.

Places of Interest Nearby

There is much to see and enjoy in *Scarborough* including the harbour, the castle, sea fishing and boat trips, as well as the stately home *Ebberston Hall* (telephone: 01723 859516), the *Rotunda Museum* (telephone: 01723 374839) and the *Wood End Museum* (telephone: 01723 367326). For information on the seasonal re-enactment of the Battle of the River Plate on *Peasholm Park Lake* telephone the tourist information office: 01723 373333.

WALK 9

SUTTON-UNDER-WHITESTONECLIFFE: A MAGIC AND MYSTERY TOUR

Gormire seems always aloof and inaccessible but this tour, using field paths and lanes through the attractive village of Thirlby, takes you to its very shores. Near the water, the path is hidden by thick woodland, the lake only grudgingly lifting her purdah at the very end.

The precipice that is Sutton Bank has broken more axles than the RAC Rally, a succession of warnings like 'Thy End Is Nigh' sandwich boards solemnly lining the route from Thirsk. A preoccupation with the mechanical usually diverts attention from the local scenery and, except for gasps of 'We made it!' and a cursory glance at one of the best views in the North of England, motorists tend to check their dials and move on, while below the wall of rock known as Whitestone Cliff, Gormire Lake slumbers on.

Looking towards Whitestone Cliff

This tour begins in Sutton-under-Whitestonecliffe, a 'last chance saloon' sort of a village where you can take on fuel and Dutch courage to equip you for the road ahead. The Whitestonecliffe Inn sits firmly at the roadside offering restaurant and bar meals and ultra-modern chalet style accommodation at the rear. Two interconnecting low-beamed bars with exposed stonework and rustic prints offer a wide choice of bar meals, the typical blackboard menu including grilled lamb cutlets, gammon and eggs, pork fillet with creamy mushrooms, steak and kidney pie, scampi, fresh Whitby haddock and more exotic choices such as honey glazed duck in a brandy and orange sauce and fillet beef stroganoff. The ale tally is John Smith's, Webster's and Tetley Smoothflow bitters backed up by Foster's lager and Guinness. Opening times from Monday to Sunday (not open Monday lunchtime except on bank holidays) are 12 noon to 3 pm and 7 pm to 11 pm (10.30 pm on Sundays). Telephone: 01845 597670.

- **HOW TO GET THERE:** Sutton-under-Whitestonecliffe is about 3 miles east of Thirsk on the A170 Thirsk to Scarborough road.
- **PARKING:** Park in the inn car park.
- **LENGTH OF THE WALK:** 4½ miles. Map: OS Landranger 100 Malton and Pickering or Outdoor Leisure 26 North York Moors - Western area (inn GR 485825).

THE WALK

1. Turn left from the inn using the footway alongside the A170 for 200 yards and go left again over a stile, following a public footpath sign. Continue going forward by the trout pond and swing right, turning left over a stile. Cross the Sutton Beck on a footbridge and keep forward fenceside, crossing a third stile in the corner. Continue alongside a wood and cross a fourth stile, walking on hedgeside. Steer diagonally right over the next field to find a fifth stile in the corner and cross right. Keep hedgeside to the next corner and cross a sixth stile through a gap in the hedge. Keep to the high ground above the beck, following the hedge to the corner, then steering diagonally right over the field to the corner. Cross a seventh stile and walk on hedgeside to a gate. Go through to a lane.

To the right of the gate is a simple memorial to Alf Wight - James Herriot - the author of 'All Creatures Great and Small'. He lived in Thirlby.

2. Turn right into Thirlby. Continue through the village to the left-hand

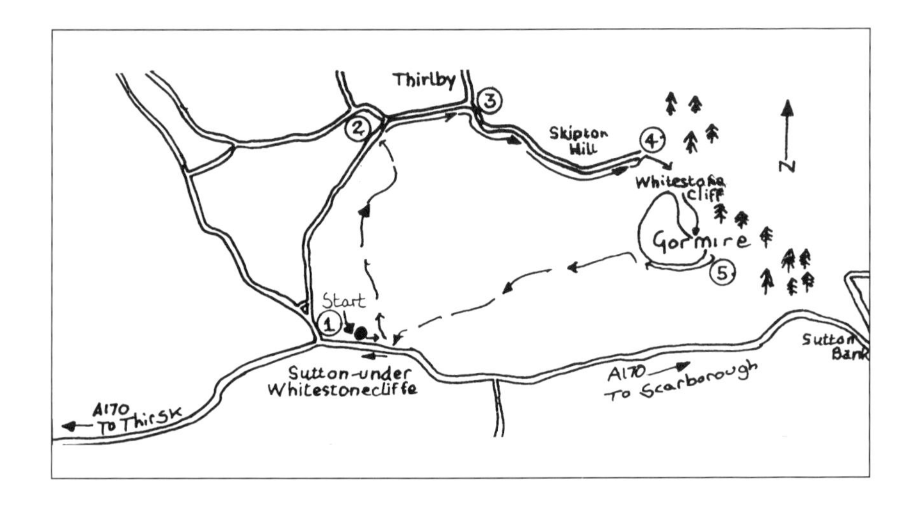

bend and steer left near the cabinet maker's shop and above the ford to the Sutton Beck bridge.

Like me, can you resist the invitation to take the weight off your pins? The inscription on the wayside bench reads: 'No shop or inn is there here about, so why not sit down and enjoy summat for nowt?'

3. Turn sharp right by Little Beck cottage and continue left by Kiln House on the quiet lane, gradually climbing.

The strange pterodactyl-like creatures above are gliders from nearby Roulston Scar.

Continue, going forward and upward past Skipton Hill and Cleaves Barn, and swing left towards the mass of Whitestone Cliff.

4. At the end of the public road, go right on a woodland track, then go right again, following the signpost to Gormire. Continue on the path alongside the lake.

Gormire's inaccessibility only adds to the mists of myth and legend that in all seasons surround it. Oval shaped and about a mile in extent, the lake is supposed to be bottomless and have no outlet and it is said to hide the remains of a once beautiful city. One local story predicts that when the lake becomes covered in hay, the White Mare of Whitestone (another local legend, associated with a plunge over the cliff by a horse) will carry it off on its back. Equally implausible is the tale of a goose. The hapless bird once sailed into the gully below the cliff and was lost. Several days later it reappeared 12 miles away in Kirkbymoorside. It was still squawking but had lost all its feathers.

The fringes of the lake are home to several rare plants. Bog bean was once collected from here for use in botanical medicine.

5. Keep going straight forward away from the lake - the right arcing turn following the shoreline is boggy - to a gate. Arc hard right, back towards the lake on a path, and follow the lake edge. Halfway along the lake path, fork left on the path uphill away from the lake through bracken. Swing right on a rough track on a parallel line with the shore and drop down, going left away from the lake on a gradually improving path. Follow the path down, looping right and hard left to a stile. Cross right and continue forward uphill, heading for a marker post in a meadow. Drop down left to twin stiles, cross and steer right for the edge of a wood. Go right and cross a stile, following the footpath sign, and dropping down to another stile. Cross and go left over a field near the caravan park to a track. Swing left on the lane to the A170. Turn right on the footway, back to the inn.

Places of Interest Nearby

In Thirsk there is the *James Herriot Museum*. In Kilburn (south of Sutton-under-Whitestonecliffe) you can see the *White Horse,* a 228 foot high horse cut into the hillside in 1857, and the *Mouseman Visitor Centre* (telephone: 01347 868222), a carved mouse being the trademark of the internationally acclaimed furniture maker Robert Thompson. Further south, at Coxwold, you will find *Shandy Hall* (telephone: 01347 868465), the former home of author Laurence Sterne, and *Newburgh Priory*, a charming old house (telephone: 01347 868435).

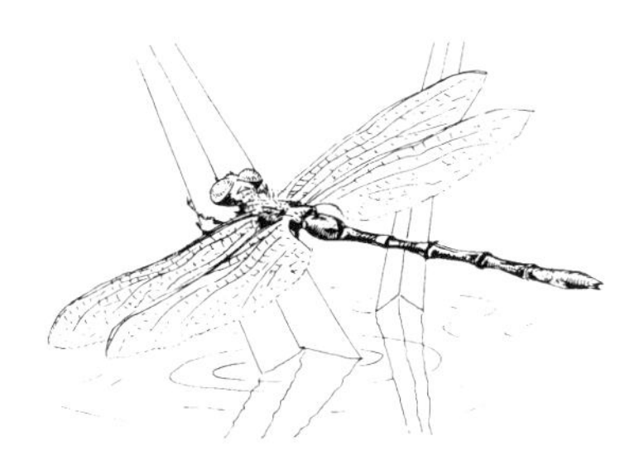

WALK 10

MALTON: CURVING THE MEAD

Roman generals and English kings, holy canons, poets and novelists and some of the fastest legs that have ever graced the turf - we will follow in their hoof marks, revelling in those wooded Derwent banks that so delighted Dickens. This is a walk of varied watery tempos. The solemnly beautiful but ponderous Derwent proceeds at the pace of a funeral march. The upstart Menethorpe Beck in contrast tumbles and dances a merry Highland Fling shouting 'Get a move on old man!' where the two waters collide.

The Derwent above Low Hutton

At a strategic crossing of the Derwent between the North York Moors and the Wolds, Malton has been a place of importance since the time of the Brigantes. The Romans came here and founded the military and civil settlement of Derventio, the town had a Norman castle and a Gilbertine priory and in more recent times it became an important cattle market and brewing centre. With the coming of the motor age and the vogue for seaside holidays, constricted Malton, however, became a town of dread. Happily, a modern bypass now relieves the strain of heavy traffic. There are many visitor attractions in the town, not least a number of old fashioned shops such as game merchants and rope makers. Malton also has a fascinating museum and a tourist information centre. Perhaps its biggest claim to fame though is its association with horse-racing. More properly any bloodstock rosettes belong to the sister town of Norton on the left bank of the Derwent. This was the home of the legendary John Scott, 'the Wizard of the North', who trained sixteen St Leger winners, six Derby winners and eight winners of the Oaks. Thoroughbreds are still trained on the nearby Langton Wold and it is rare for walkers hereabouts not to encounter some steed being put through its paces. Take a pocket book and pencil. There is also a turf accountant in the town.

The walk commences in the centre of Malton opposite the King's Head Hotel in Market Place. An attractive and distinctive double-gabled building re-erected in 1908 after a disastrous fire, the King's Head looks across to the ancient Bull Ring and St Michael's Church. Behind is Malton's colourful cattle market. The King's Head has a popular light and airy front parlour decorated with rustic photographs and prints. In contrast, tucked away to the rear is an intimate and cosy panelled back-bar warmed by an open fire in winter. Recite the stockman's password to get in.

The hotel which has bed and breakfast accommodation and an upstairs restaurant serves bar meals at lunchtime and in the evenings. Blackboard specials such as roast topside of beef, lamb's liver and onions and salmon fillet are a daily feature of the extensive menu which includes hot beef and chicken club sandwiches, seasonal quiches and fresh fish. The King's Head is noted for its real ales, the wide and frequently changing choice of beers typically including Deucher's India Pale Ale, Wexford Irish Cream, Marston's Pedigree and Deakins Golden Drop, together with Stella Artois and Carling lagers. Opening hours are 11 am to 3 pm and 7 pm to 11 pm from Monday to Saturday. Sunday hours are 12 noon to 3 pm and 7 pm to 10.30 pm. Telephone: 01653 692289.

- **HOW TO GET THERE:** Malton is north-east of York and is easily accessed off the A64 trunk road.
- **PARKING:** Pay and Display car parking is available opposite the King's Head. Alternatively, motorists may park free of charge in the large car park in Norton (the walk passes this car park). It is located just south of the level crossing on Bruntwood Terrace.
- **LENGTH OF THE WALK:** 6½ miles. Map: OS Landranger 100 Malton and Pickering (inn GR 786716).

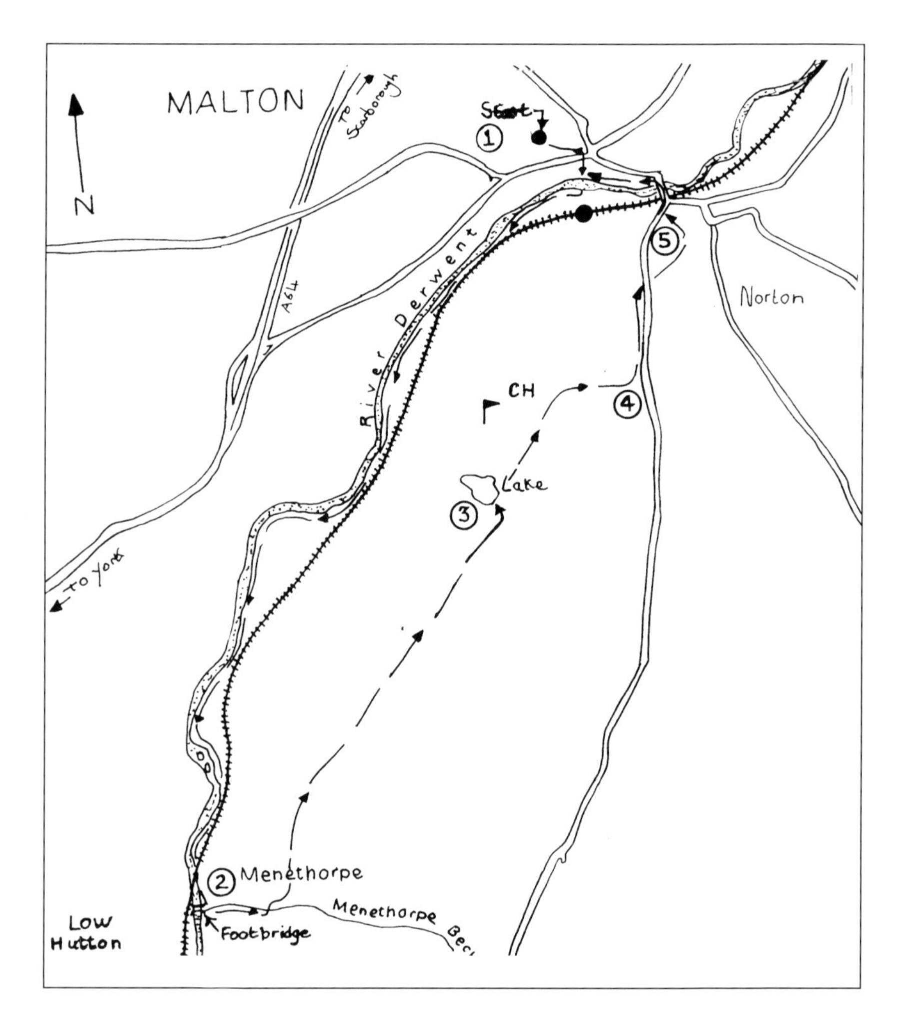

THE WALK

1. Turn right along Market Place, walking downhill on Norton Road towards the river. Cross the Derwent bridge and go immediately right along Riverside View. Swing to the right of the play area and keep going straight forward through the gate on the riverside path, following the yellow arrow marker.

From this footpath you will see grand period houses on the right bank and, above a loop of the river and its inviting Cherry Islands, the village of Low Hutton. Watch out for a medley of birds including

Canada geese, mallards, shelducks, moorhens, and kingfishers.

Continue for about 3 miles then pass under the railway bridge and walk on for about 250 yards to the suspension bridge.

This was erected in 1855 by the London and North Eastern Railway Company to enable the villagers of Menethorpe to use Low Hutton station.

2. Swing left away from the river on a path and go left again on the quiet road, arcing right alongside the Menethorpe Beck. Go left over the beck and follow the road past Menethorpe Hall, continuing to the next bend. Keep going straight forward on a track, following the public footpath sign. Drop down on a woodland track and leave the beech wood, crossing a stile and walking on alongside the golf course for about 400 yards.

3. Turn sharp left, following a fence, and walk on towards Welham Hall lake. After about 200 yards go right across a stile, steering left to the paddock corner. Cross a further stile and walk left over an arched bridge, following a track through the golf course. Go to the left of the clubhouse, cross the car park and find a public footpath at the left-hand side of the access road. Go left over the stile and swing right to the road.

4. Go left using the footway and turn right into Lakeside Gardens, crossing the feeder stream bridge and swinging left. Turn right at the end of the lake, following a winding public footpath and turn left to the Bruntwood Terrace car park.

5. Continue to the junction and turn right to the level crossing, swinging left across the railway lines to Norton Road. Turn left for about 120 yards and go right, following the public footpath along the side of the Derwent to the bridge. Turn right over the bridge, back to the starting point.

Places of Interest Nearby

Malton Museum (telephone: 01653 695136) with its interpretation of Wharram Percy deserted medieval village (*Wharram Percy* itself is to the south-east, off the B1248). *Eden Camp* (telephone: 01653 697777) is a fascinating place to visit, with 29 former POW huts covering multiple aspects of the Second World War.

WALK 11

WELBURN: THE GRANDEST TOUR

With the imperial cry of peacocks on the wind and stunning vistas that evoke the magnificence of ancient Egypt, Greece and Rome, this surreal tour through part of the Castle Howard estate has the dreamlike qualities of a sleepwalk. Where else would you encounter a castle, a pyramid, a temple and a tomb whose combined cost in the 18th century must have exceeded the national debt?

Alongside streams and through a bluebell wood to a sumptuous arched bridge over a lake, our walk beguiles us with a visit to the Temple of the Four Winds and a meeting with Vespasian, Trajan, Faustina and Sabina. The other magnetic attractions are views of the flag-fluttered castle and an orbit of the enormous Mausoleum.

The Crown & Cushion at Welburn.

Welburn is a satellite village to Castle Howard whose owners often frowned on licensed premises. Lucky then that the Crown & Cushion, a 300-year-old former farmhouse, survived the final towel draping that condemned the neighbouring village of Coneysthorpe to dry cups. The inn has an interesting name derived from the actions of the landlord of the erstwhile Wagon and Horses who celebrated the arrival of Queen Victoria in the district by placing a crown on a cushion outside his premises. He celebrated the royal visit by renaming his inn and commissioning a new sign. Enlarged in recent years to include a restaurant and an attractive beer garden, the cosy yet spacious inn has a snug bar and extensive dining areas decorated with themed pictures and photographs of Scarborough. The constantly changing menu includes dishes such as beef in a beer casserole, lamb steaks with Greek salad and pitta bread, chicken curry, chicken in cider sauce, Whitby haddock, smoked salmon, home-made steak and kidney pie, grilled gammon and mushroom and asparagus pancakes and vegetable lasagne. The house ales are Tetley and Camerons Strongarm supported by Carlsberg lager. The inn is open from 11.30 am to 3 pm and 5.30 pm to 11 pm on Monday to Friday. Weekend hours are 11 am to 11 pm on Saturdays, 12 noon to 10.30 pm on Sundays.

Telephone: 01653 618304.

- **HOW TO GET THERE:** Welburn is between York and Malton and is easily reached off the A64 near Barton Hill.
- **PARKING:** Park in the inn car park or on the roadside.
- **LENGTH OF THE WALK:** 5 miles. Map: OS Landranger 100 Malton and Pickering (inn GR 720680).

THE WALK

1. Turn left from the inn along the street for 150 yards and go left just after the War Memorial building, down Water Lane. Veer left on a track at the side of the pumping station, following the public bridleway sign. At the field corner keep going forward, heading for Pretty Wood.

This wood lives up to its name, especially in spring when it is a blue haze of flowers.

2. Enter the wood through a gate and drop down to cross a stream, continuing uphill left. At the edge of the wood, go through a gate, following the Centenary Way sign on a track.

To the left is the Pyramid built in 1728. Inside, it has a beehive vault and a colossal bust of Lord William Howard, founder of the Castle Howard dynasty. On the right, the Mausoleum comes into view.

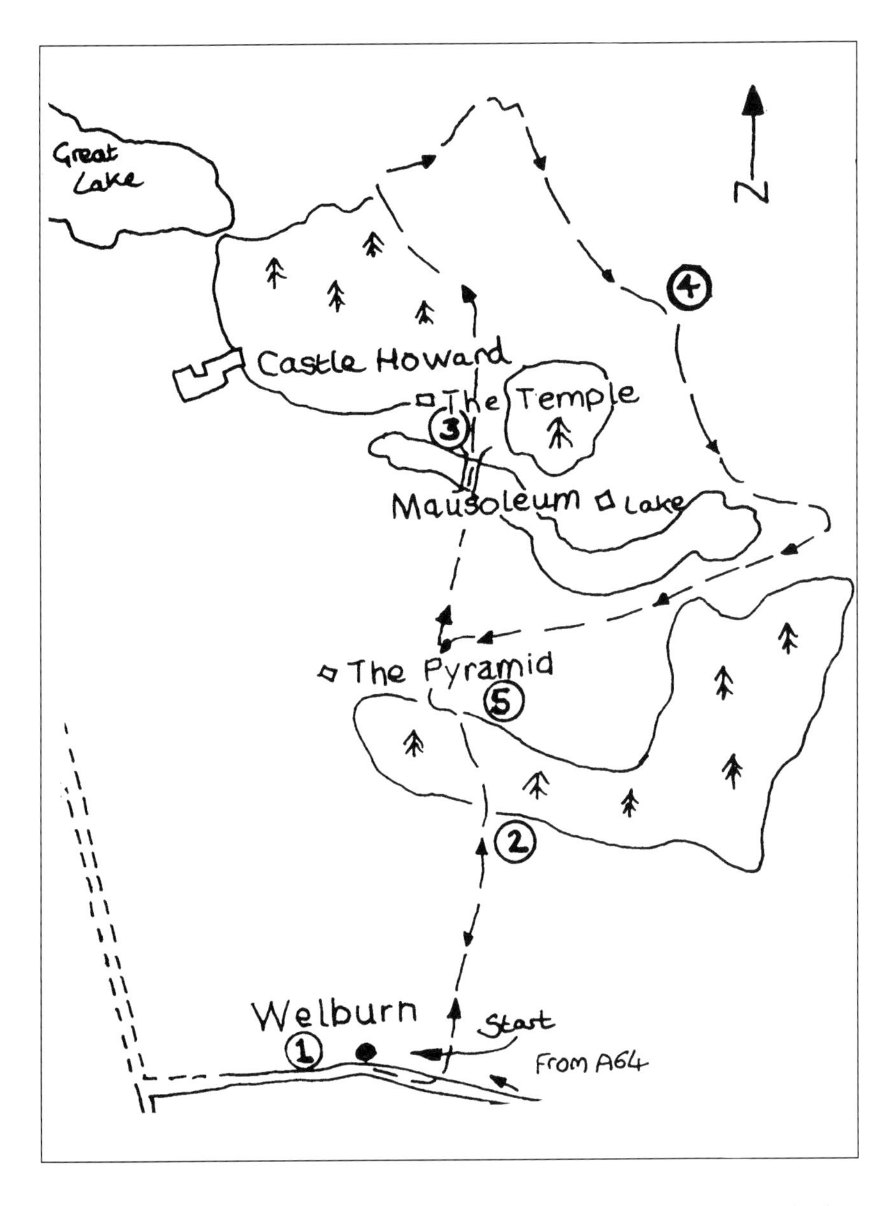

Horace Walpole suggested that it may tempt you to be buried alive such is its opulence. In terms of size and cost, it has been compared with Wren churches in the City of London. Sited on a hill overlooking the lake, the building has 20 Tuscan columns and rises to a prodigious height. It took 11 years to build.

Continue to the farm road and turn left for 30 yards, turning right on a signposted path towards the bridge.

This three-arched span was erected around 1744. From its parapets, beyond a waterfall, you can see Castle Howard in all its glory. A monumental theme park built for the third Earl of Carlisle, Castle Howard was begun in 1700 to the designs of Vanbrugh, a Captain in the Marines who had no architectural experience!

3. Cross the bridge and go left to the side of the Temple of the Four Winds.

Dating from 1724-26, and again by Vanbrugh, the temple takes its design inspiration from the classical Villa Capra.

Continue on the green track alongside the estate boundary wall to a gate. Go left over a stile, following a yellow arrow marker, swinging left to the Centenary Way sign.

4. Turn right here along a track, swinging left to cross a stream. Swing right uphill towards Bog Hall and turn right, following the signs on the barn on a path to the side of the farmhouse. Follow the track left, going left and right across a stream. Walk on left to the farm buildings and go right to the road.

5. Turn right and go left on the track back into Pretty Wood, retracing your steps to the inn.

Places of Interest Nearby

Castle Howard and its gardens (telephone: 01653 648333). The remains of *Kirkham Priory*, the other side of the A64. *Sheriff Hutton Castle* (ruins) is to the south-west of Welburn, and *Nunnington Hall* (NT), a 17th-century manor house with gardens (telephone: 01439 748283) is north-west of Malton, off the B1257, not far from the attractive village of *Hovingham*.

WALK 12

FLAMBOROUGH: ON THE TRAIL OF SMUGGLERS, PIRATES AND A SWALLOWED TOAD

Show any schoolboy a map of England and he will immediately recognise the raven's beak that is Flamborough. The distinctive chalky head which juts out into the North Sea was once fluttered by the infamous raven standard of the Norsemen and their legacy lives on in local placenames and in the longship-inspired design of the fishing cobbles which still ply their trade from North Landing.

Using centuries-old tracks, our route visits the inlet of South Landing and climbs the steep cliffs to the southernmost flank of Danes Dyke and its nature reserve.

North Landing

With its lighthouse, ancient castle, 12th-century church, secret coves, honeycombed caves and a roll-call of heroes that includes Flodden veteran Sir Marmaduke Constable and John Paul Jones the pirate, Flamborough has a history to inspire a whole shelf full of yarns. One such book is the neglected *Mary Anerley* by R. D. Blackmore: 'At the furthermost edge of the cave, however, the craggy basin had a lip of flinty pebbles, just enough for a bather to plunge from; but it ran across the broad edge of the cavern, and from its southern corner went a deep dry fissure mounting out of sight into the body of the cliff. And here the smugglers were merrily at work.'

For over 300 years, from smugglers to their Serene Highnesses the Prince and Princess Louis of Battenburg who gave the inn its name after a visit in 1900, the Royal Dog and Duck has had a colourful succession of customers. Fishermen still frequent the fo'c'sle-like bar, and there are three cosy additional rooms and two patio areas for the summer months. Welcoming and attractively decorated with marine photographs, the inn has a robust value for money menu which gives star billing to 'sizzling steaks' - beef, pork and gammon. Home-made steak pie, dressed crab and the freshest of fish dishes are very popular with tourists. The house ales are Bass, Stones, John Smith's and Caffrey's bitters complemented by Bass mild and draught Guinness. Daily opening times are 11 am to 11 pm (10.30 pm on Sundays). Telephone: 01262 850206.

- **HOW TO GET THERE:** The inn is in Dog and Duck Square, Flamborough. Its rear entrance is off the B1255 north-east of the church. Flamborough is well signposted from Bridlington along the B1255.
- **PARKING:** Park in the inn car park, on Dog and Duck Square or on nearby High Street.
- **LENGTH OF THE WALK:** 3½ miles. Map: OS Landranger 101 Scarborough and Bridlington area (inn GR 227706).

THE WALK

1. Turn right from the inn over Dog and Duck Square and go left down Allison Street, swinging right on South Sea Road to the junction. Cross, following the signs to the Heritage Centre on South Sea Road, going left towards the sea. Pass the Heritage Centre (open Easter to Autumn) and drop down on the road to the cove - South Landing.

The new lifeboat station here replaces the one at North Landing.

2. Turn right, going up the steep cliff steps, following the sign to 'Danes Dyke'.

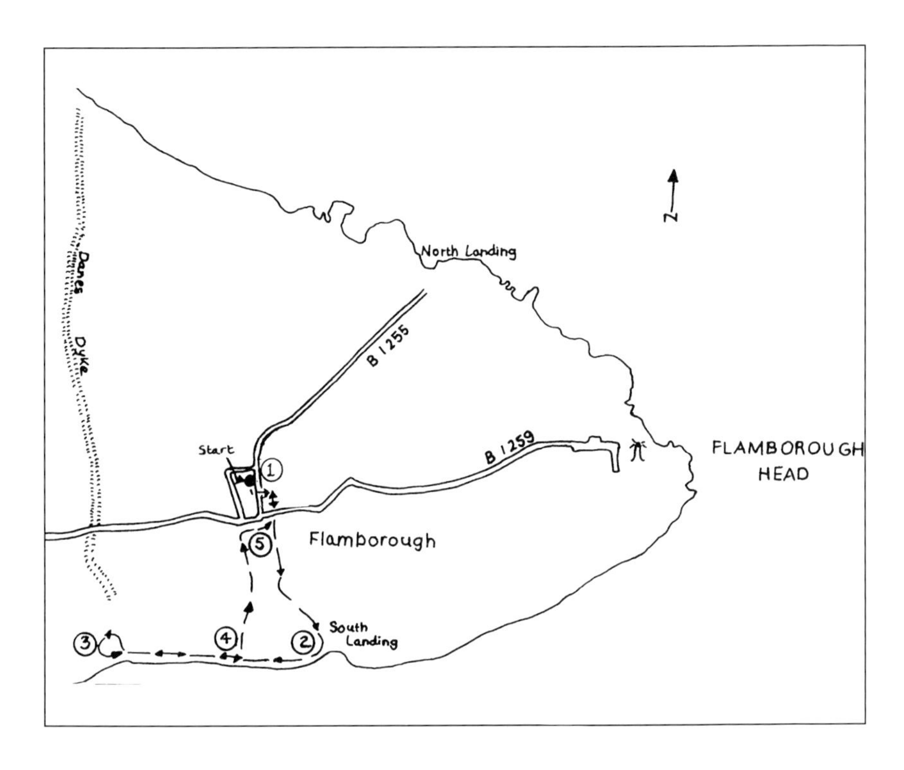

Nearly 3 miles long, this defensive work effectively severs the promontory and encloses an area of some 5 square miles. It was originally attributed to the Vikings and for many years the locality was known as Little Denmark. Today it is thought to date from the Iron Age.

Continue along the headland path.

The skirmish between 'Father of the American Navy' John Paul Jones and the English navy took place off the cliffs to the left during the Battle of Flamborough Head in September 1779.

Pass the Second World War pill box and drop down a steep ravine on the steps, rising again on the steps and continuing along the cliff-top path to the wood. Weave right through the fringe of trees to the signboard and go right on a well-defined gorse-lined path away from the sea. Drop down steps and swing left into the nature reserve of Danes Dyke.

South Landing

Blackmore writes beautifully of its charms: 'Humble plants which had long lain flat stood up with a sense of casting something off; and the damp heavy trunks which had trickled for a twelve-month, or been only sponged with moss, were hailing the fresher light with keener lines and dove-coloured tints upon their smoother holes. Then conquering the barrier of the eastern land-crest, rose the glorious sun himself, strewing before him trees and crags in long steep shadows down the hill. Then the sloping rays, through furze and brushland, kindling the sparks of the dew, descended to the brink of the Dyke, and scorning to halt at petty obstacles, with a hundred golden hurdles bridged it. . . .'

3. Turn left along the path, downhill towards the sea and the cove. Turn left up the steps and climb the cliff, retracing your steps along the headland path to the signpost to Flamborough.

4. Turn left here, following the fenceline, and swing right, following the yellow arrow marker, going left in the field corner towards Beacon Farm. Go over a stile by the gate and cross the farmyard. Swing right on West Street, walking on towards the church tower, and continue on Butlers Lane, going right past the church.

Dating from around 1150, the church of St Oswald - he is the patron saint of fishermen - is a little jewel. Sir Marmaduke Constable who was the trusted servant of several kings from Henry VI to Henry VIII has his tomb in the church. On top of the tomb is a skeleton, the still visible rib cage revealing an engorged heart and a curious lump of stone, said to be a petrified toad. Legend suggests that Sir Marmaduke swallowed the toad whilst drinking, the creature devouring his heart until it died. Of even more interest is the Flamborough Book of Service displayed on a sort of carousel. This description does scant justice to a stirring series of framed plates that open up like butterfly wings from a central pivot to reveal one man's tribute to the many Flamborians who saw service during World War II.

5. Continue past the church and go left on South Sea Road, making your way back to the inn on the outward route.

PLACES OF INTEREST NEARBY

From April to September, there is the outstanding spectacle of 200,000 nesting seabirds including puffins and gannets at *Bempton Cliffs Nature Reserve* (telephone: 01262 851179). *Bridlington* offers many attractions and at the north-east end of the town you will find *Sewerby Park and Hall* with its exhibitions, zoos and gardens (telephone: 01262 677874).

WALK 13

BISHOP WILTON: A SPRING LINE TODDLE

Not far from the infamously steep Garrowby Hill, this sometimes strenuous toddle ascends towards the highest point on the Yorkshire Wolds. From a vantage point of over 800 feet, York Minster, the Pennines and the White Horse of Kilburn are all visible. Springs are the lifeblood of the villages and dales that occupy the chalky northern flanks of the Yorkshire Wolds. The limestone landscapes of the north-west of the county are justly famous, but how many people have ever even heard of the villages of Bishop Wilton, Great Givendale, Millington and the delightful surrounding valleys of Worsen Dale, Church Dale, Given Dale, Mingle Dale, Whitekeld Dale and Wan Dale? Wearing our divining-rod boots, we will explore each of the three seldom visited villages, seeking out the nearby dales and their delicious spring waters.

Bishop Wilton

In a crevice of a steep escarpment, Bishop Wilton is a rock flower splashed by a merry beck, its tendril roots firmly bedded into the sinuous valley that is Worsen Dale. Careering and bubbling unimpeded through the village, the beck forms the prettiest of pictures framed by a curvaceous border of grass and lines of old red-tiled cottages that hug its length. Opposite the school at the top of the village, Bishop Wilton once had a sumptuous archbishop's palace, used as a summer residence by the incumbents of York. Its moat can still be seen. Higher up the pastures are the intriguingly named Hagworm Wood and Stonetable Hill. Wooden swords in hand, can the children find the mythical hagworm or the place where Aslan the lion was sacrificed? Down the street is St Edith's church. Begun by the Normans, it was exquisitely restored by Sir Tatton Sykes. Its floor, a replica of one in the Vatican, is a gem.

In the centre of the village is the welcoming Fleece inn. Popular with walkers, it has a public bar, a small restaurant and a parlour-type room packed with hunting trophies, clocks, brasses, old paintings, photographs and general paraphernalia commemorating the rustic history of Bishop Wilton. On one wall is the tin sign taken from the premises of Fishers Agricultural Engineers who kept their forges burning just across the way for over a century. In the restaurant is one of the firm's bicycles - a penny-farthing. The homespun menu is big on steaks and Sunday roasts, other dishes including a generous mixed-grill - customers are vetted for their big appetites - home-made steak and kidney pie, scampi and plaice. Ask for egg and chips and rather quaintly you will be served a pickled egg in a bag of crisps! On tap are Tetley and John Smith's bitters and Kronenbourg and Foster's lagers. Draught Guinness is also available. The inn is open on Mondays from 7 pm to 11 pm. Opening hours for the rest of the week are 12 noon to 2 pm and 6 pm to 11 pm. Telephone: 01759 368251.

- **HOW TO GET THERE:** Bishop Wilton is best accessed from the A166 York to Driffield road. Turn off at the foot of Garrowby Hill on the signposted lane.
- **PARKING:** Park in the inn car park or on the side street.
- **LENGTH OF THE WALK:** 8 miles. Map: OS Landranger 106 Market Weighton and surrounding area (inn GR 797551). It should be noted that following a Diversion Order, the route in point 6 differs from that shown on the OS map.

The Walk

1. Go straight forward from the front door of the inn up the street, following the beck. Where the road swings left at the top, veer right (the yellow arrow sign is on a post), following the beck almost to the front door of a cottage (number 78). Go right up the grassy bank, following the public footpath sign and continue arcing right to a track. Follow the track right and then walk along Park Lane, going down to the road. Turn left out of the village, continuing on the road for 300 yards and going left to a spring and a public footpath sign.

2. Cross the stile and ascend the hill, keeping to the side of the hedge.

Like Darwin, you may discover fossil stones underfoot. Sea shell specimens are fairly common on this hillside and it is at this point that the grand panorama unfolds itself.

At the summit go right along the crest and follow a winding path left up a short incline to a stile. Cross and walk on for 80 yards to a stile. Cross right and continue along the edge of a field, going left in the corner for 200 yards to a stile. Cross right and walk on, dropping down into a dip and rising. Continue to a gate, going through left on a farm track between hedges. Swing right through a second gate into the village of Great Givendale. Go left on the road to the junction with Beacon Road.

Church Dale is over the road on the left. Mingle Dale and Deep Dale are behind. In front, in a sylvan little dell, is the church of St Ethelburga overlooking three inter-connecting lakes.

3. Cross the road and go forward through the iron gate, descending on a path to the church (if you want to visit, the door is usually open). Go left through a gate and swing right on a path, walking on above the lakes. Continue to a gate and drop down into the bottom of the valley, following a stream. Walk on, arcing right to a bridge over the Whitekeld Beck.

The beck is fed by the Swirlingmoor and White Keld springs up Whitekeld Dale to the left. The margins support a diversity of wild flowers including marsh marigold, figwort and yellow flag.

4. Keep straight forward up the bank at the side of the wood and go over the meadow to a stile. Cross and turn right towards the farm

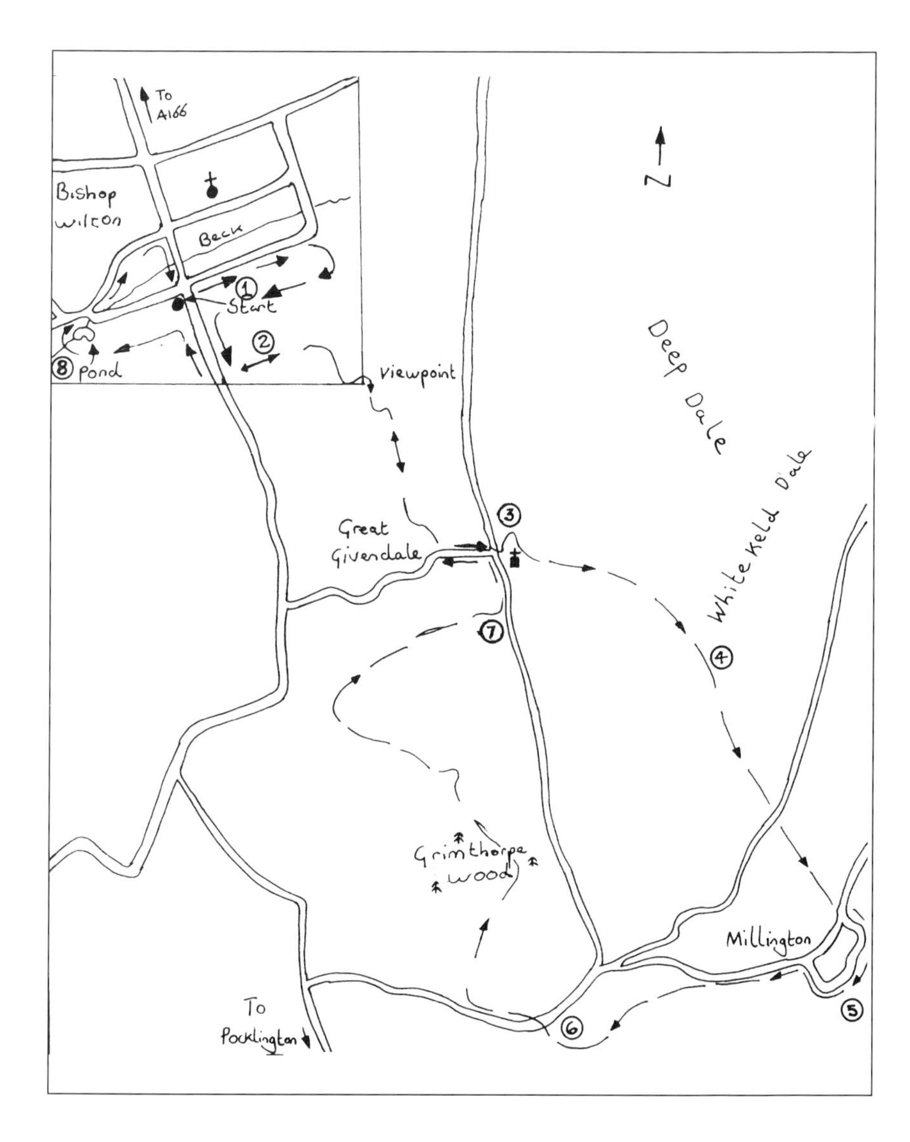

buildings, going left by a barn and continuing on a track to the road. Cross and continue on a quiet lane, dropping down towards Millington. At the junction, cross and again drop down, swinging right into the village.

At weekends, Millington has a choice of refreshment options: the Rambler's Rest Tearoom - cosy, offering home-made fare - and the Gate Inn, which is also open on weekdays.

5. Continue through the village, arcing right uphill to the quiet lane. Go left. At the bend follow the public footpath marker. At the metal gates, fork right between field boundaries and steer left along a hedgeline, following a yellow arrow marker. At the corner, go right towards a farm and veer left, crossing a stile to a farm access road. Turn right and pass a pond, continuing to the lane.

6. Merge with the lane left and walk on to the bend, going right past Ousethorpe Farm down Miller Lane. After 300 yards, go right over a stile, crossing a large field and aiming for double telegraph poles, then steering left for a prominent white direction sign on a tree at the edge of Grimthorpe Wood. Cross a stile into the wood and follow the yellow arrow marker right, leaving the wood and going left. The Diversion Order takes effect from this point. Walk along the edge of the wood to the field corner and follow the yellow arrow marker right for 100 yards. Go left over a stile, weaving right to a footbridge across a stream, then go left over a stile hedgeside for 200 yards to the field corner, continuing along the hedgeline at the top of the steep bank for about ⅓ mile to the corner of the very large field. Turn right in the corner and follow the fenceline up and generally left towards a wood. In the field corner, go right for about 200 yards and cross a stile left into a wood, turning right on a path, continuing for about 200 yards to a stile and the road.

7. Cross and go left on the road, walking on past the Givendale sign for about 450 yards. Go left opposite the church and retrace your steps back over the wold to Bishop Wilton. Once past the village sign, go left down South Lane, keeping straight forward on a cart track.

8. Cross the beck (an old mill once stood here – today it's a newly established nature reserve) and swing right on the lane, following the beck back to the inn.

Places of Interest Nearby

The *Rocking Horse Shop* (small museum and manufacture) in Fangfoss, south-west of Bishop Wilton (telephone: 01759 368737). *Burnby Hall Gardens* in Pocklington has one of the finest displays of waterlilies in Europe (telephone: 01759 302068). Gliding is possible at *Pockington Airfield* (telephone: 01759 303599).

WALK 14

YORK: AN OUSE AND FOSS AMBLE

Waterside Walk Cocktail: Take the zest of one of Europe's finest cities, add a double slug of river, a tincture of lake and a dash of fountain. Infuse the whole mixture in a vessel that has seen more water than a submarine. Shake, stir and serve on a warm summer's day. Invigorating!

The historic inn at the start of the walk

The city of York has, of course, visitor charms aplenty. This leisurely amble, for the most part, leaves the attractions and the thronged precincts behind, taking a weaving route along the Ouse and Foss esplanades and through two municipal gardens. A sensuous walk full of the sounds, sights and smells of a busy waterway – dawdlers may well get shanghaied by the local cruiser captains – it presents an amazing array of architecture. Is there anywhere in England – nay the world – that in such a short compass can present buildings from a thousand years of history?

Historically, the King's Arms on King's Staith is one of the most famous public houses in Britain. Flooding apart, it is linked to Richard III who is reputed to have used the nearby wharf for disembarkations to the royal seat in Middleham Castle. Practically built with stone floors and exposed brick walls it has one L-shaped room warmed by open fires in winter. During the warmer weather its seating capacity is more than doubled by the addition of outside tables. Meals are served at lunchtime only, the standard menu, supplemented by daily specials such as home-made game pie, including roast beef and giant Yorkshire puddings, gammon, steaks, lasagne, haddock and a selection of filled baguettes. Samuel Smith's beers and lagers (not forgetting a range of speciality cocktails!) complement the food - Old Brewery Bitter, Extra Stout, Ayingerbrau Pils. Opening times are 11 am to 11 pm from Monday to Saturday. Sunday hours are 12 noon to 10.30 pm. Telephone: 01904 659435.

- **HOW TO GET THERE:** The very prominent King's Arms is on King's Staith near Ouse Bridge in the centre of York.
- **PARKING:** Pay and Display parking is available close by but York gets very congested especially during the summer months and I would recommend using the excellent 'Park and Ride' facilities available on the outskirts of the city at Grimston Bar (Hull Road), Askham Bar (A64) and Clifton Moor (A19). Cheap services operate every 10 minutes (telephone: 01904 431388 or 707726).
- **LENGTH OF THE WALK:** 2½ miles. Map: OS Landranger 105 York and Selby (inn GR 603517).

THE WALK

1. Turn left from the inn and continue along the river bank to Skeldergate Bridge. Go left up the steps and turn right over the bridge. Go hard left in an arc, dropping down back to the river. Turn right and continue along the Ouse path to the entrance to Rowntree Park.

The park was given to the citizens of York by the famous confectionery firm of Rowntrees to commemorate the contribution of its workers to the 1914-18 war effort.

2. Turn right and walk through the park, going through the gateway and over the bridge which separates the lake. Turn right and fork left leaving the park by a side gate. Swing right down Lovell Street, go left

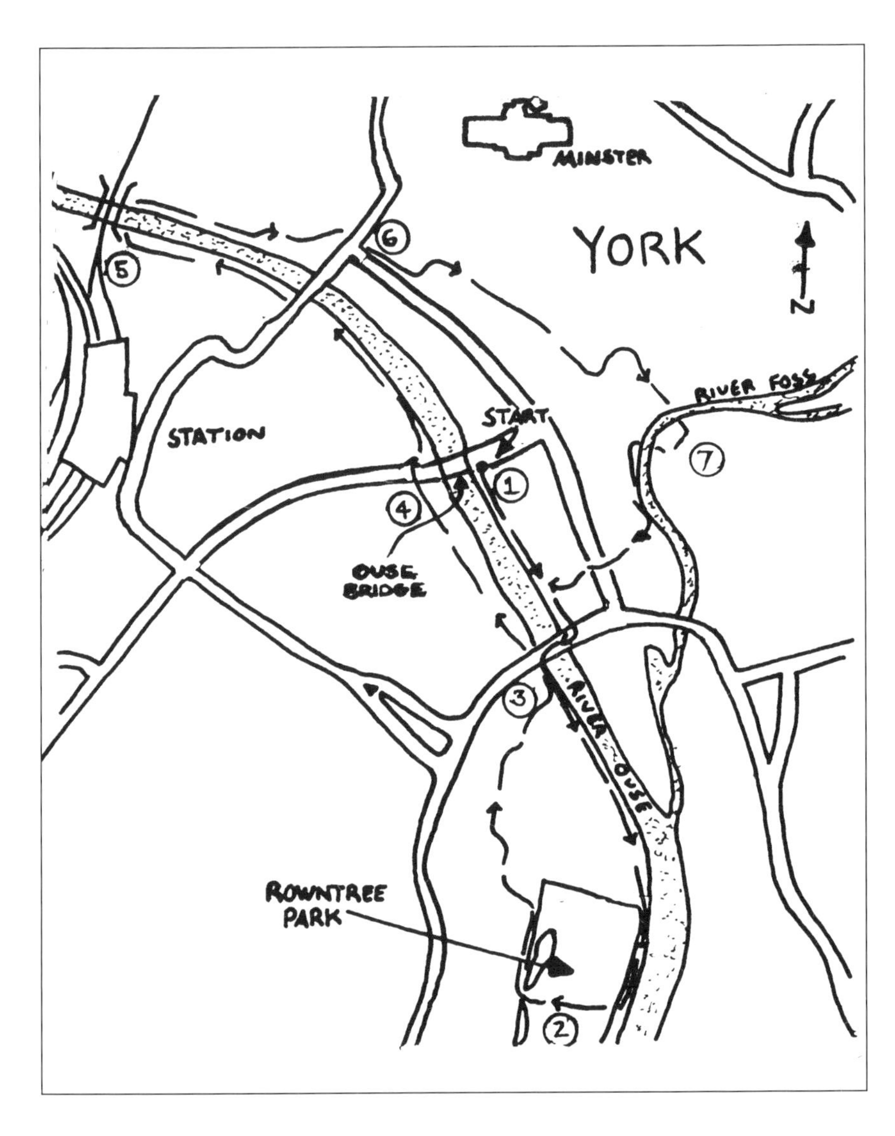

and right along Teck Street. Drop down the steps and walk through the alleyway, turning left by the Clementhorpe Centre and go next right along Bridget Court and Cherry Street. Turn right and go first left by the Slip Inn along Postern Close, weaving right, left and right again back to the Ouse bank. Turn left upstream.

3. Continue under the bridge and proceed along Skeldergate.

There are a number of interesting old buildings on this street - particularly the Bonding Warehouse of 1875 and the Ann Middleton Hospital (rebuilt in 1829 but the original statue at the front dates from 1659). See also the Brass Rubbing Centre.

4. Turn right on Bridge Street - do not cross the bridge - and go left along the riverside footway, passing through a garden. Swing right by the General Accident Building and continue under Lendal Bridge on the riverside path up to the railway bridge.

5. Go right, using the footbridge alongside the railway line, cross the river and turn right, walking downstream. Pass Marygate and the old tower and go left through a gate into the Museum Gardens, following the winding path up right to the entrance gates.

To the left is the ten-sided Multangular Tower. Part of the Roman fortress, it is one of the best Roman structures in Britain. It was erected in the 4th century, possibly under the direction of Constantius Chlorus who died in York in AD 306.

6. Cross the road and walk along Lendal, going left over St Helen's Square (very quickly to avoid the scrumptious debaucheries of Betty's Café) and right down Davygate. Continue along Parliament Street passing the fountain and, at the corner, turn left on Pavement. Turn right along Fossgate.

This road passes over the Ouse's diminutive sister - the 15 mile long river Foss. It was once an important commercial artery for the city and the villages beyond.

7. Turn right on Merchantgate and go right again on Piccadilly over the bridge, turning left on the signposted path alongside the Foss. Go left, weave right by the side of Cliffords Tower and cross the road into the park, turning right, back to the starting point.

PLACES OF INTEREST NEARBY

There is so much to see and do in York. The *Minster* is the largest medieval cathedral in northern Europe (telephone: 01904 624426) and at the popular *Jorvik Viking Centre* visitors are 'whisked' back 1,000 years in 'time cars' (telephone: 01904 643211).

WALK 15

ATWICK AND HORNSEA: SHORELINE PADDLE – MERESIDE STRADDLE

Our route here follows the beach - there is nothing more de-stressing than this! - into the attractive seaside resort of Hornsea and leads on through the town to the shores of the picturesque Hornsea Mere.

On the western edge of the mere, the path uses the entrance to Wassand Hall. With the sun twinkling through the leaves, the joyous experience of marching down this drive under an honour guard of tall cinnamon coloured beach trees is worth a chest full of medals.

Atwick

Such is the rate of erosion of the soft glacial clay cliffs hereabouts, that the shoreline is slowly receding and, in time, the village of Atwick will itself be endangered. For now though, it endures, preserving its sea-cobbled cottages, village green and an ancient stone cross.

An old coaching inn, the Black Horse stands alongside the coast road overlooking Atwick's village green. Adapted in recent years to the tourist trade, it offers a commodious lounge bar and a smart dining area.

Photographs of local scenes and characters liven the walls of both rooms, one picture showing a knot of men smoking fish at the back of the inn in Victorian days. The standard menu of bar meals features fresh haddock, home-made steak pie, mixed grill, steaks, gammon, chicken curry and a range of vegetarian dishes. A real ale inn, the Black Horse serves guest beers and John Smith's and Tetley bitter, together with Foster's and Beck's lagers. Opening times from Monday to Friday are 11.30 am to 4 pm and 6 pm to 11 pm. Saturday hours are 11.30 am to 11 pm. Sunday opening is 12 noon to 10.30 pm. Telephone: 01964 532691.

- **HOW TO GET THERE:** Atwick is some 2 miles north of Hornsea on the B1242.
- **PARKING:** Park round the village green.
- **LENGTH OF THE WALK:** 8 miles. Map: OS Landranger 107 Kingston upon Hull and surrounding area (inn GR 191509).

THE WALK

1. Go left from the inn towards the village cross.

In 1786, this was recorded as being 3 miles from the sea. Now, the distance is less than ½ mile.

Turn right, following the sign to the seafront, down Cliff Road. Follow the road round left past the duck pond. (Second World War pill boxes are to the left.) Before the erosion warning sign, turn right into the caravan park and go left on the track towards the cliffs.

2. Scramble down to the beach when it is safe to do so and go right towards distant Hornsea. Continue along the beach to the Marine Hotel and walk up the slipway, continuing along the sea wall to a second slipway, turning right along New Road.

3. Go left through the Memorial Gardens and leave the gardens at the end, turning right on Burton Road. Steer right by Tranmere Park and go left, forking right up the steps onto the track of the abandoned railway. Turn right and follow the path, dropping down to a main road and a roundabout. Cross to Marlborough Avenue straight ahead and walk down this cul-de-sac avenue to the next right-hand turn, turning right just past the school sign on a signposted path. Go through the allotments and turn left along the road for 250 yards, turning right

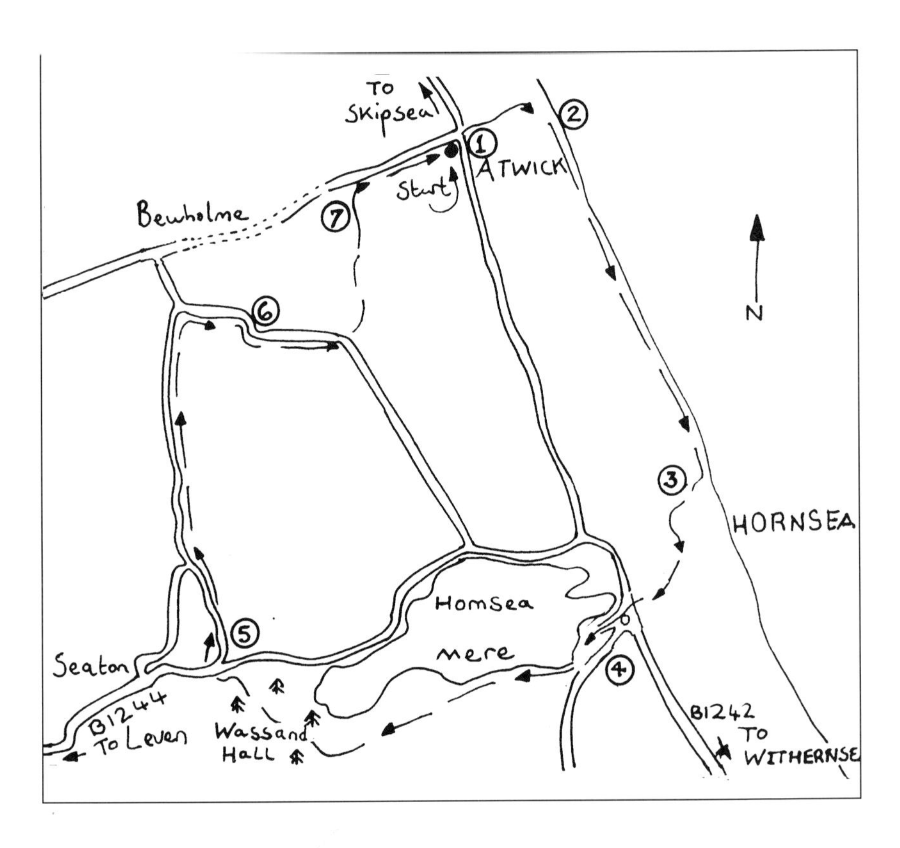

following a sign 'Hornsea Mere Walk.'

If, like me, you have circumnavigated the perimeter of Hornsea Mere with just one oar, you will realise that it is the largest freshwater lake in Yorkshire at 1½ miles long by ½ mile wide. It is a nature reserve and abounds with fish and waterfowl. So prolific was the harvest of pike and roach in the 13th century that a tournament to settle the disputed fishing rights was fought between the monks of St Mary's in York and those at Meaux Abbey. In 1260, the monks and their champions clouted each other round the lugs all day with staves, the final victory going to York.

4. Aim left across the water meadows away from the mere edge to a kissing gate. Go through and, keeping to the bottom of the bank, go forward to the edge of the field, following the arrow marker hedgeside on a path between two fields. Go through a series of kissing gates, following the waymarkers, and turn right on a bridleway track through a gate into the grounds of Wassand Hall. Pass the hall (built in 1813) and continue down the spectacular drive to the road.

5. Cross the road to the footway and go left for 150 yards, turning right on the quiet country lane, signposted to Bewholme. Continue along this lane for about 1½ miles and go right on the lane signposted to Hornsea.

6. Pass Little Arram and, at the next bend, go left, following the footpath sign along a hedge-line to the corner. Turn left on a path between two fields, heading for a deserted farmhouse. Follow the path right and left round the farmhouse perimeter hedge and merge right with an access track, swinging right and left to a stile.

Next to the stile is a memorial to seven airmen who lost their lives during an ill-fated flight on 20th February 1944.

7. Cross and turn right on the lane, continuing into Atwick, back to the inn.

Places of Interest Nearby

Boating and fishing are possible on *Hornsea Mere*. In Hornsea itself you will find *Hornsea Museum*, with exhibitions of rural life (telephone: 01964 533443) and *Hornsea Freeport Shopping and Leisure Village* (telephone: 01964 534211).

WALK 16

SUTTON UPON DERWENT: MEANDERING

Once renowned for lampreys and salmon, the picturesque Derwent is one of the most important rivers in Yorkshire, supplying nearly 20% of the county's water needs. Striding the boundaries of two ridings, this walk visits the frequently flooded ings around Sutton upon Derwent and Elvington, the inundations creating an ideal habitat for water birds. But watch out for submerged stiles! The voluptuous arching bridge and curvaceous river are as seductive as a Saharan soda-fountain, attracting hundreds of anglers and scores of boats especially in summer. Walkers can also enjoy the old lock-keeper's house and the cool fringes of Sutton Wood.

A path along the Derwent.

Until the 14th century, Sutton upon Derwent could be accessed from the west only by a ford or a ferry at high tide. Today, an elegant honey-coloured bridge dating from 1700 links the village to Elvington and the tidal flows have been tamed by downstream flood barriers and lock-gates. Massive abstraction works take Derwent water via pipeline to all parts of Yorkshire. As well as the interesting church of St Michael - prudently perched on a ridge overlooking the river - the village possesses an old manor house and two pubs, one of which marks the start of our walk.

Constructed from old ships' timbers, the inviting St Vincent Arms has four cosy rooms (one, the small restaurant room, is non-smoking), elegantly furnished and decorated in period style with corner cupboards and delph racks. Open fires in winter, home-cooked food and a range of real ales given a CAMRA accolade add to the attractiveness. Typical offerings from a menu that changes daily include speciality steak and kidney pie, pork fillet in a cream sauce and breast of wood pidgeon with port and redcurrant. Other game and fresh fish dishes feature from time to time. Up to ten quality ales may be on tap on any day, a typical line up including Fuller's Chiswick Bitter and London Pride, Charles Wells Bombardier, Timothy Taylor Landlord and Old Mill Bitter from the local Snaith Brewery. Lager choices are Kronenbourg and Foster's. Opening hours from Monday to Saturday are 11.30 am to 3 pm and 6 pm to 11 pm. Sunday hours are 12 noon to 3 pm and 7 pm to 10.30 pm. Telephone: 01904 608349.

- **HOW TO GET THERE:** Sutton upon Derwent is on the B1228, about 5 miles south-east from its roundabout junction with the A1079 at Grimston east of York. The access from the south, via junction 37 of the M62 and north through Howden on the B1228, makes for a leisurely rural drive with little traffic.
- **PARKING:** Park in the pub car park or on-street.
- **LENGTH OF THE WALK:** 3 miles. Map: OS Landranger 106 Market Weighton and surrounding area (inn GR 707474).

THE WALK

1. Turn left from the inn along the footway, passing the village hall on the main street.

This unassuming building has an inspirational history, owing its existence to a resourceful former rector. He came to the village in 1921 and devised a unique fundraising scheme asking well-known authors to contribute passages from their works for publication in an annual birthday calendar. The Reverend Pimm raised the money,

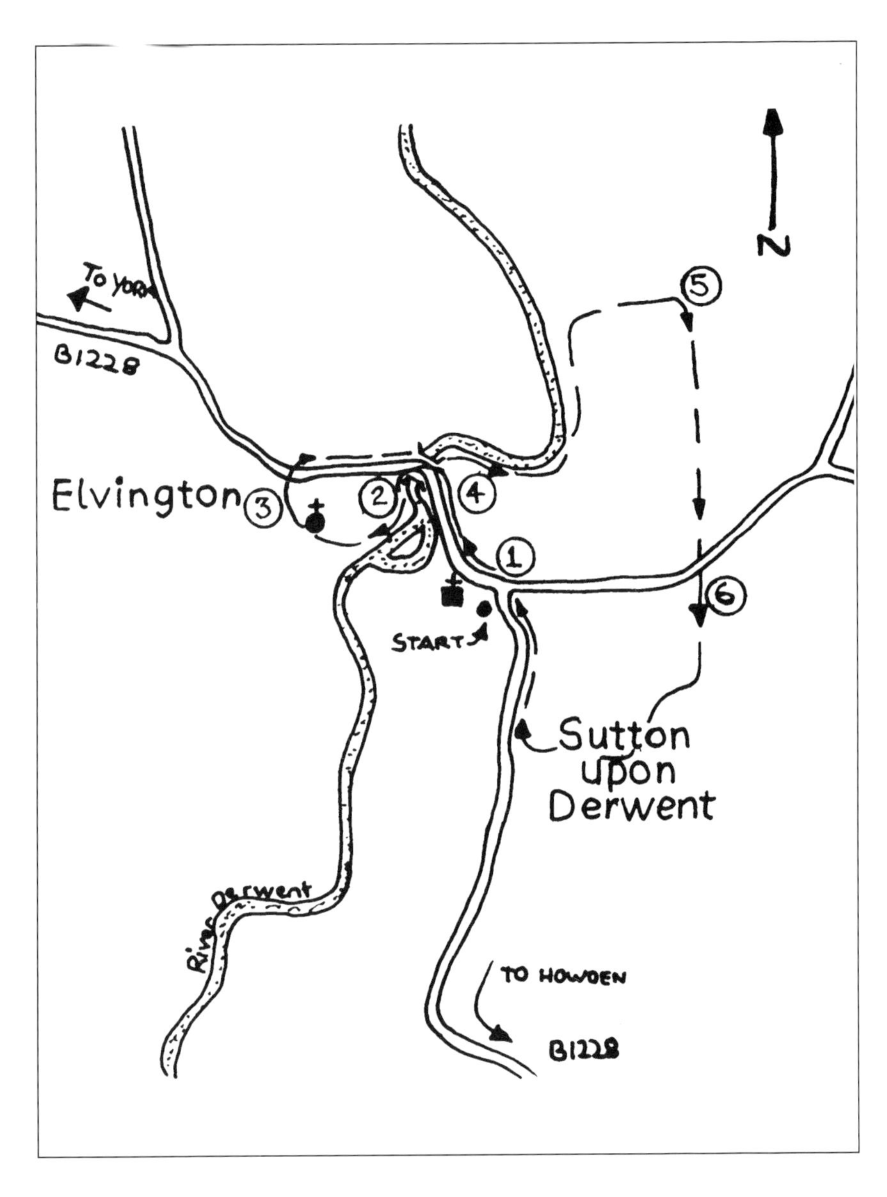

dug the foundations, laid bricks, fastened wood and tiled the roof, completing the building with help from local people in 1931.

Continue on the footway and pass St Michael's church on the bend.

The St Vincent Arms in Sutton upon Derwent.

Much rebuilt, the church has some intriguing fragments, notably the massive 11th-century arch in the north wall of the chancel. Rediscovered in 1927, this arch shows a battered figure of St George spearing a dragon. Elsewhere in the church, does the inscription to Sir John Jervis, Admiral of the Fleet in Napoleonic times, have any connection with the St Vincent Arms? Is his ship depicted on the inn sign?

Walk on and pass the derelict mill. (Access to the lock-keeper's house is along the footbridge over the unusual guillotine-action lock.) Continue to the bridge. On a post on the left-hand side of the bridge is a push button traffic light control to allow horseriders and pedestrians safe access over the bridge - use this and walk over the bridge, going immediately left on a footpath along the river bank.

2. Continue past the lock-keeper's house to the lock and go right through the gate, following the fenceline down to the corner of the field. Keep going forward across a footbridge and walk up to Elvington's Holy Trinity church (built to the design of William White in 1877). Swing right, go through a kissing gate and continue past the church on Church Lane to the B1228.

3. Turn right on the footway and walk back to the bridge, using the traffic light control near the premises of Geoff Stubbins (ironworks) to re-cross.

4. Turn immediately left, following a footpath marker over a stile and down some steps, swinging right along the river bank. Follow the path left, go through a kissing gate and at the next kissing gate, steer right 45° to a third kissing gate at the edge of Sutton Wood. Go through and cross a stile, following a public footpath sign uphill along the fringe of the wood. Keep going forward at the next sign, crossing a footbridge and weaving right to a fourth kissing gate. Go through and keep straight forward, leaving the wood along a track for about 150 yards.

5. About 25 yards beyond a post, turn sharp right, following the footpath sign on a path between two fields, continuing to the road.

6. Turn right for 100 yards and go left hedgeside, following the public footpath sign to the field corner. Go left at the post and arc hard right, following the marked path along a hedge line. At the corner, go left at the signpost, continuing to a track. Turn right along the track into Sutton upon Derwent. Turn right, back to the inn.

Places of Interest Nearby

At Elvington there is the *Yorkshire Air Museum*, a memorial to the allied air and ground crews of the Second World War (telephone: 01904 608595). Good walks can be had in *Allerthorpe Wood* (east of Sutton upon Derwent) and along the banks of the *Pocklington Canal*. The various attractions of *York* (see walk 14) are only a few miles away.

WALK 17

LONDESBOROUGH AND GOODMANHAM: A WOLDS WAY WANDER

Presenting an attractive landscape of gently folded chalk hills and dry valleys, the Yorkshire Wolds are noted more for aridity than wetness. Our walk, however, discovers a surprising medley of water features, the circular track linking two old lakes, a number of streams and a holy well.

The lakes bridge near Londesborough.

Historically, this compelling ramble spans a thousand years, treading an old Roman road, pilgrim tracks dating from the time of King Edwin and two abandoned railway lines. Londesborough and Goodmanham are connected by ancient footpaths and by a momentous event in English history that brought Christianity to a kingdom that stretched from Yorkshire to the Forth.

Despite the demolition of its 70-roomed mansion in 1818, the elevated estate village of Londesborough continues to radiate considerable charm. A pinnacled and many chimneyed replacement hall beams out over the sweetest of valleys, and, on the hillside nearby, hidden behind some of the largest yew trees in the riding, is the 12th-century church of All Saints and the neatly ordered village. Many of its buildings bear the intertwined cypher of Lord Londesborough. This timeless place, which had a population in 1377 of just 65 taxpayers, has the rhythm of a grandfather clock and a current roll call of around 200 souls.

Our walk begins outside the Londesborough Tea Garden in Top Street. This deliciously relaxing establishment has won local accolades for its cream teas, dainty sandwiches and home-made cakes, and is open from the beginning of May to the end of August on Fridays, Saturdays, Sundays and Mondays from 11 am to 4 pm. Telephone: 01430 873347.

Halfway through the walk, in Goodmanham, is the Goodmanham Arms, an old fashioned and wonderfully real pub, the adjective describing the ale, open fires and the genuineness of the welcome. Serving Black Sheep and Theakston bitters together with Murphy's stout and Carlsberg lager, the pub is open from 7 pm to 11 pm Monday to Friday. On Saturdays and Sundays the opening hours are 12 noon to 4 pm and 7 pm to 11 pm. Hot roast beef and pork sandwiches are available on Sunday lunchtimes. Telephone: 01430 873849.

- **HOW TO GET THERE:** Londesborough is 2 miles north of Market Weighton and can be accessed using the A1079 and the A164.
- **PARKING:** Roadside parking is available on Top Street in Londesborough.
- **LENGTH OF THE WALK:** 6½ miles. Map: OS Landranger 106 Market Weighton and surrounding area (cafe GR 868456).

THE WALK

1. Proceed north-eastwards along Top Street to the junction and turn right, following the 'Wolds Way' sign downhill. Continue downhill on a woodland track, passing the entrance drive to Londesborough Hall. Go through a gateway and follow a footpath marker left over a stile and across a field to a second stile in the valley bottom. There is a lake and a merry cascade to the left. Cross and walk uphill, steering to the right of the big tree. Cross a third stile and continue going forward, dropping

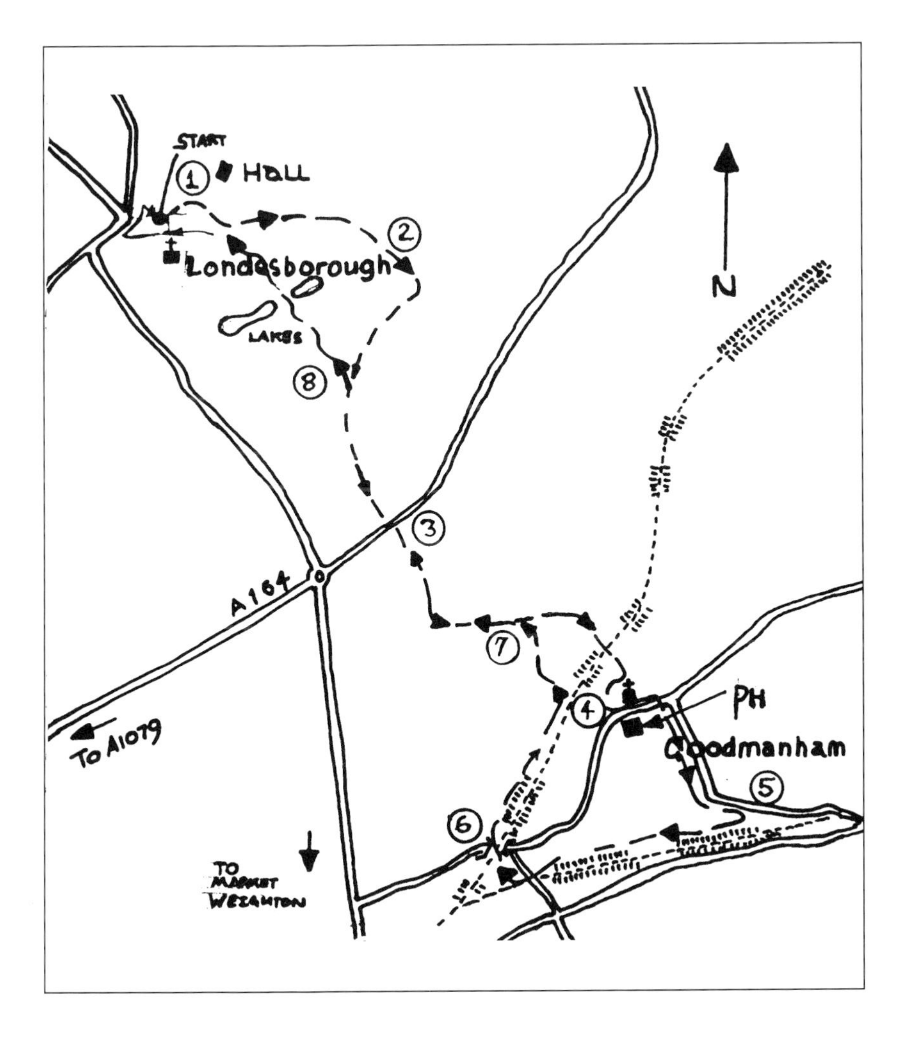

down and heading for the farm buildings on the far side of the valley. Go through a kissing gate, cross a footbridge over a stream in the bottom and cross a fourth stile.

The field to the left marks the site of the medieval village of Easthorpe demolished between 1720 and 1740 to enlarge the deer-park. Fifty yards from the stile, at the top of the hill, is a series of bumps delineating the route of the Roman road between Brough and Malton.

2. Aim right, for the edge of the woodland, crossing pastureland to a fifth stile. Cross and turn right along a farm road, gradually walking uphill and veering left to the crest.

Southwards, the long distance view takes in the distinctive hilltop church of All Saints, Holme-on-Spalding-Moor. For hundreds of years its landmark tower acted as a beacon for travellers braving the surrounding bogs.

Keep going left and at the right-hand bend go forward along a hedgeside path to the road.

3. Cross the road, swing right by the layby/picnic area and go left, following the 'Wolds Way' sign along the edge of a field. Turn left in the corner and continue on a track, dropping down and swinging right under an old railway bridge uphill into Goodmanham. Turn right past the church.

Of largely Norman origins, the exquisite church of All Saints is built on the site of a pagan temple destroyed by the chief priest Coifi. Together with King Edwin, he was converted to Christianity by Paulinus who preached at the famous Great Council of Northumbria held at the royal court in Londesborough in the year AD 626.

4. Go left to the Goodmanham Arms and then left again uphill for 200 yards.

On the left, propped up against the wall just beyond the entrance to Manor Farm, notice the old milestone.

Turn right along the quiet back road, following the 'Wolds Way' sign. Drop downhill, going left into a valley aptly named on the old maps as Spring Dale and gradually converge with an abandoned railway line. Look out for a culvert on the right and turn right just beyond it over tussocky grass, scrambling up onto the track of the former Market Weighton to Beverley railway line.

The route is now known as the Hudson Way after George Hudson, the 'Railway King', a former owner of the Londesborough estate.

5. Turn right. Walk on for about 600 yards, inspecting, to the left, the bubbling St Helen's Well.

The spring water issuing from the bank above has long been regarded in the locality for its spiritual and therapeutic properties.

Walk on for a further 200 yards and go right down the steps into a nature reserve, turning left along the banks of the stream for 300 yards. Turn left up the steps back onto the track and turn right for a few yards, going left up the steps at the side of the bridge. Turn right on Red Lane over the bridge, continuing past the Goodmanham sign over the stream to the junction. The house to the right was the former village mill. Turn left along the footway, following the stream down to the bridge.

6. Go left on a path up the embankment and turn right onto the abandoned railway track. Walk on for about ½ mile and, almost opposite Goodmanham, look out for a small bridge over an old trackway. Turn left just before the bridge on a winding path through the fringe of trees, weaving right and swinging left on a green track between two fields. Continue to a marker post and go right along a hedgeline arcing left around the field corner.

7. Walk straight ahead, re-treading the outward path with the hedge to your left, continuing to the next field corner. Turn right to the road and follow the outward route back on the hedge path and the farm road to the 'Wolds Way' sign.

8. Go left over a stile into Londesborough Park, dropping down and arcing left to the lakes. Cross a second stile and a footbridge over a stream between the lakes.

Originally dug around 1730, these lakes support a wide diversity of wildfowl including mallards, teals, tufted ducks and Canada geese.

Cross a third stile and go forward uphill, swinging left through a gateway to a track. Turn right.

The vaulted terrace wall to the left gives some indication of the grandeur of the original hall. During the Second World War stained glass from York Minster was removed to these vaults for safe-keeping.

Londesborough Park

Continue uphill, going through the gate left into the village. Go left along Low Street past the church to the corner.

It is interesting to deviate a few yards, going forward to inspect the E-shaped building that was the old hospital. It was founded in 1680 to accommodate 'six old men and six old women' and endowed with £100 per year charged to the Londesborough estate.

Turn right and right again, back to Top Street.

PLACES OF INTEREST NEARBY

The hilltop church at *Holme-on-Spalding-Moor*, off the A164 south of Londesborough, and the charming estate village of *South Dalton*, north-east of Goodmanham.

WALK 18

TADCASTER AND NEWTON KYME: LOOPING THE LOOP

Smothered in flowers in summer, this gentle route leads to the former Roman station at Newton Kyme. Covering some 10½ acres, the fort on the south side of the river was built in the 4th century. Near the still visible fragment of rampart wall is the wonderfully kept 13th-century church of St Andrew and the imposing Newton Hall.

Bridge Street, Tadcaster.

This ale, it is a gallant thing,
It cheers the spirits of a king,
It makes a dumb man strive and sing,
Aye, and a beggar play!
A cripple that is lame and halt,
And scarce a mile a day can walk,
When he feels the juice of malt,
Will throw his crutch away.

This old Craven Churn Supper song could well be the anthem of Tadcaster, whose streets, in all seasons, are pungent with the 'juice of malt'. Three breweries dominate modern Tadcaster, a town that developed from the Roman garrison of Calcaria into a strategically placed coaching centre. Our walk begins at an old coaching inn, the atmospheric Angel and White Horse whose celestial and equine attributes include my all time favourite quaff and shire horses stabled in the rear yard. But before we sample its wares, let us earn our thirsts! We will loop the loop, not as a consequence of over imbibing, but as a result of following the Wharfe, leaving the acrobatics to its sand martins. Never has travelling round in circles been more leisurely.

With both a painted sign and sculpted wings, the Angel and White Horse is the most prominent building in Bridge Street and the attached brewery, which has been run by the staunchly independent family firm of Samuel Smith since 1758, is the oldest such enterprise in Yorkshire. Caparisoned inside with quality panelling, the inn is simply but elegantly furnished, photographs of the brewing trade decorating its walls. Intimate corners on different levels offer cosy dining, with an al fresco option in the adjacent brewery coachyard. Displayed on a blackboard, the menu of home-made meals is changed daily, traditional fare dominating. Try the roast topside of beef, honey roast ham, liver and sausage casserole, steak and kidney pie, spotted dick or ginger and lemon sponge washed down by a tipple that may account for that pile of crutches in the corner. Out of the famous Sam Smith stable, Old Brewery Bitter is a very special brew. Of similar pedigrees are its stablemates, Sovereign, 4x and Ayingerbrau lager. The inn is open on Monday to Friday from 11 am to 3 pm and 5 pm to 11 pm. Saturday opening is 11 am to 4 pm and 7 pm to 11 pm (no food on Saturdays). Sunday hours are 12 noon to 3 pm and 7 pm to 10.30 pm. Telephone: 01937 835470.

Nearby on High Street is another refreshment thoroughbred. Sample the 'legendary quiches' in Clare's Pantry.

- **HOW TO GET THERE:** Tadcaster is betwixt Leeds and York off the A64.
- **PARKING:** Free municipal parking is available behind High Street (entrance down the one-way Chapel Street).
- **LENGTH OF THE WALK:** 4 miles. Map: OS Landranger 105 York and Selby (inn GR 486434).

The Walk

1. Go straight forward from the inn, crossing Bridge Street and walking down Kirkgate, then veer right through St Mary's churchyard to the river Wharfe.

The church was frequently inundated in the past. Modern levees help stop the flooding.

Turn left along the bankside track. Cross the stile by the weir and continue towards the old viaduct. Go left, following the bank under the span. Cross a stile and pass the pumping station, continuing over a stile and under a second abandoned railway line through a small tunnel. Walk on to a stream at the wide right-hand bend and go right across the concrete revetment and through a gate, following the yellow arrow marker.

2. Keeping bankside, cross a stile and a bridge over a stream to a further stile. Cross and follow the water's edge over another stile to the end of the footpath at the boundary to Newton Hall. Turn left, following the sign to the corner. Turn left again and go right on a green track in front of the church and the hall to a gate and the public highway.

Inside the little church of St Andrew is a list of vicars dating from 5th April 1289. The scratched-in figures on the porch entrance are fascinating and I also found, in a niche inside, a primitive detached bust inscribed with the date of 1613. The churchyard is no less interesting. Is the incongruously sited portal a relocated fragment of the castle window described by Pevsner? Near this fragment, intricately assembled from hand-made bricks, are two of the most unusual gravestones I have ever seen. Opposite the church is the early 19th-century Newton Hall. On the ground floor it has a seven-bay Tuscan colonnade surmounted by a cast iron verandah. The original hall was built by Admiral Robert Fairfax.

3. Retrace your steps back to the concrete revetment and go right, away from the river, and follow the path left to a stile and the road.

4. Cross and by the farm entrance gate go left, following the sign to 'Inholmes' through a 'metal curtain' gate. Steer left to cross a field and

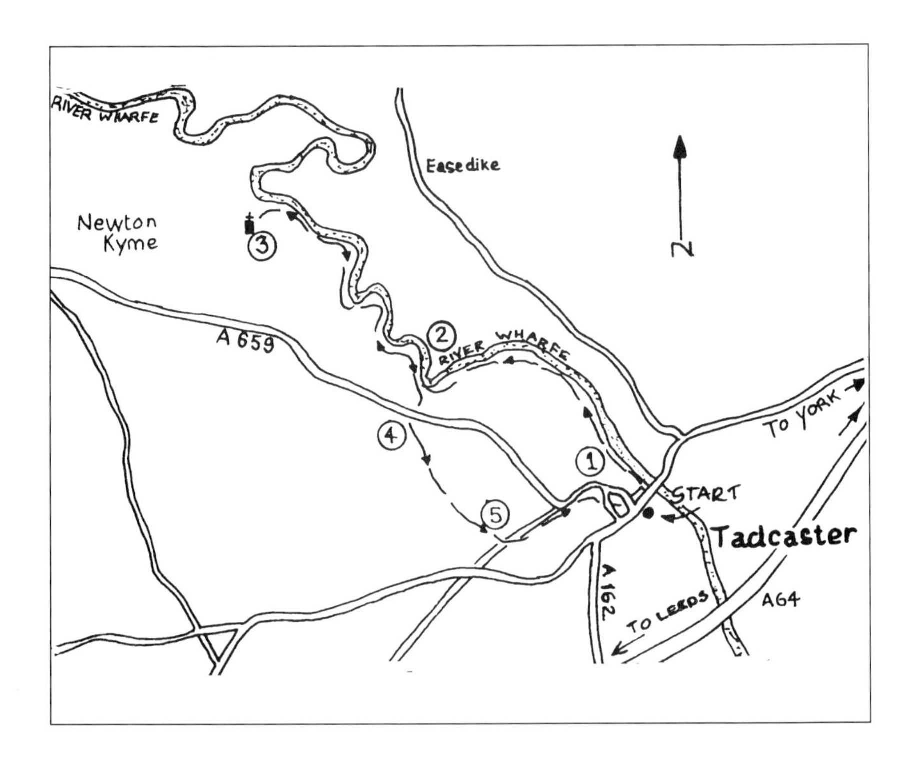

go through a second 'metal curtain' gate, swinging left on a track. Weave right then keep hedgeside left. Cross a stile and swing left and right by the horse chestnut tree to a stile. Cross, following a yellow arrow marker. Keep left over a small field and go through a wicket gate, swinging right onto Inholmes Lane.

5. Follow the lane to the road and go left opposite the fire station, walking on past the Tower Brewery. Continue going forward down Station Road, passing the swimming pool and swinging right on Westgate and Chapel Street, back to the car park.

Places of Interest Nearby

Lotherton Hall Bird Garden, with free entry to extensive aviaries, is south-west of Tadcaster, off the B1217 (telephone: 0113 2813529). In Ulleskelf, downstream from Tadcaster, you will find *John Taylor Basketmaker*, the last surviving traditional maker of baskets on the river (telephone: 01937 832138).

WALK 19

GOOLE AND HOOK: A DOCKS AND OUSE DAWDLE

Following an intriguing yellow-lined path, the route explores Goole Docks, crossing over massive lock-gates and passing some of the town's more fascinating buildings. It leads onward, alongside the well-named brown and turgid Ouse to the little known but expanding hamlet of Hook before returning through fields to Goole. There are no crocodiles in this tale but we will allude, by and by, to a whale and a sturgeon.

The Humber Promenade.

Goole, Hook and slimy Ouse. Characters from Peter Pan? No! but they are no less intriguing. When the river fogs roll in and the dockside cranes rise up like a convention of church spires there is, in this fascinating part of Yorkshire, a whiff of menace and mystery in the air, an atmosphere given added resonance in Goole by the looming presence of the empty Lancashire and Yorkshire Railway Goods Offices of 1892 and a clutch of mildly sinister wharfeside drinking dens. If press gangs still plied their trade, they would look no further than the monumental Lowther Hotel on Aire Street.

In 1820, the whole of the sparsely populated Goole area was a veritable bog. At an altitude of just 10 feet above sea level, the site of England's most sea-distant port was encircled by the Aire, Ouse and Dutch rivers and was prone to tidal flooding. By 1826, however, the rapidly developing town was linked by canal to Knottingley and it offered, in direct competition to the nearby port of Hull, a new harbour, docks and warehousing. For many years, wool exports and cotton imports formed the bulk of cargoes. With the coming of the Lancashire and Yorkshire Railway in 1848, Goole became a major transhipment centre for West Riding coal, hundreds of the colourful 'Tom Pudding' compartment boats plying their trade between pit and pier. The 1880s were probably Goole's most successful years, a combination of astute management – the inspirational W. H. Bartholomew was made chairman of the Goole Steam Shipping Company in 1880 – and well-designed and superbly built ships. During this period, the so called 'Greyhounds of the Humber' achieved a notable reputation for speed and efficiency. The funnels of these most distinctive vessels were painted black, red and buff and the GSSC became commonly known as the 'Soot, Blood and Suet Line'. Today, the port of Goole is expanding once more, its cargoes including cars and Swedish timber.

The walk begins at the Old George public house on Market Square in central Goole. Accommodation is limited to a tastefully furnished dining room, a pool room and an outside patio for use in the summer months but home-made food attracts large numbers of lunchtime diners – no evening meals and no food on Sundays. The menu is changed daily and offers a combination of regional specials such as liver and onions, steak and kidney pie and corned beef hash together with more cosmopolitan variations like penne with spinach, bacon and mushroom and seafood pasta bake. The wide range of beverages includes Stone's, Worthington, John Smith's, Bass and Caffrey's bitters, Carling Black Label lager and draught Guinness. Opening hours Monday to Saturday are 11 am to 3 pm and 7 pm to 11.30 pm. Sunday opening is 12 noon to 3 pm and 7 pm to 10.30 pm. Telephone: 01405 763147. There are also various cafés and restaurants close by.

- **HOW TO GET THERE:** Goole is easily accessible from junction 37 of the M62 at Howden. Turn left and left again onto the A614 and go south over the Ouse, using Boothferry Bridge and following the signposts back over the M62 into the town. Go left at the traffic lights and cross the level crossing by the railway station, swinging right and forking first left and left again down Stanhope Street to the roundabout. Take the third left off the roundabout, passing the Old George and the supermarket on Boothferry Road, and turn next left to the free car park which is on the right.
- **PARKING:** There is no parking at the Old George - use the public car park (see above).
- **LENGTH OF THE WALK:** 5 miles. Map: OS Landranger 106 Market Weighton and surrounding area (GR 746237).

THE WALK

1. Go right from the inn along Boothferry Road and turn right on Aire Street, continuing past the Lowther Hotel.

Built in 1827, this impressive building is one of the oldest in the town. Originally called the Banks' Hotel it was renamed in honour of Sir John Lowther who was chairman of the navigation company when the canal was opened.

Keep forward, passing on the right of the Ouse and Ship Dock's bridge between the yellow lines. Follow the yellow lines between the warehousing and swing left to Ocean Lock, going right over the lock-gates footway to Barge Dock.

On the 5th September 1884 a 9½ ton whale pushed open the lock gates and swam into this dock. The leviathan was eventually hauled onto the quayside and cut up, its skeleton being sold to the South Kensington Museum in London.

2. Go left, again following the yellow lines, and turn right into South Street, walking on to Bridge Street. Go right and cross over the bridge, using the footway.

The immensely tall structures on the left are the twin water towers (the old one held three-quarters of a million gallons) dating from 1883 and 1926.

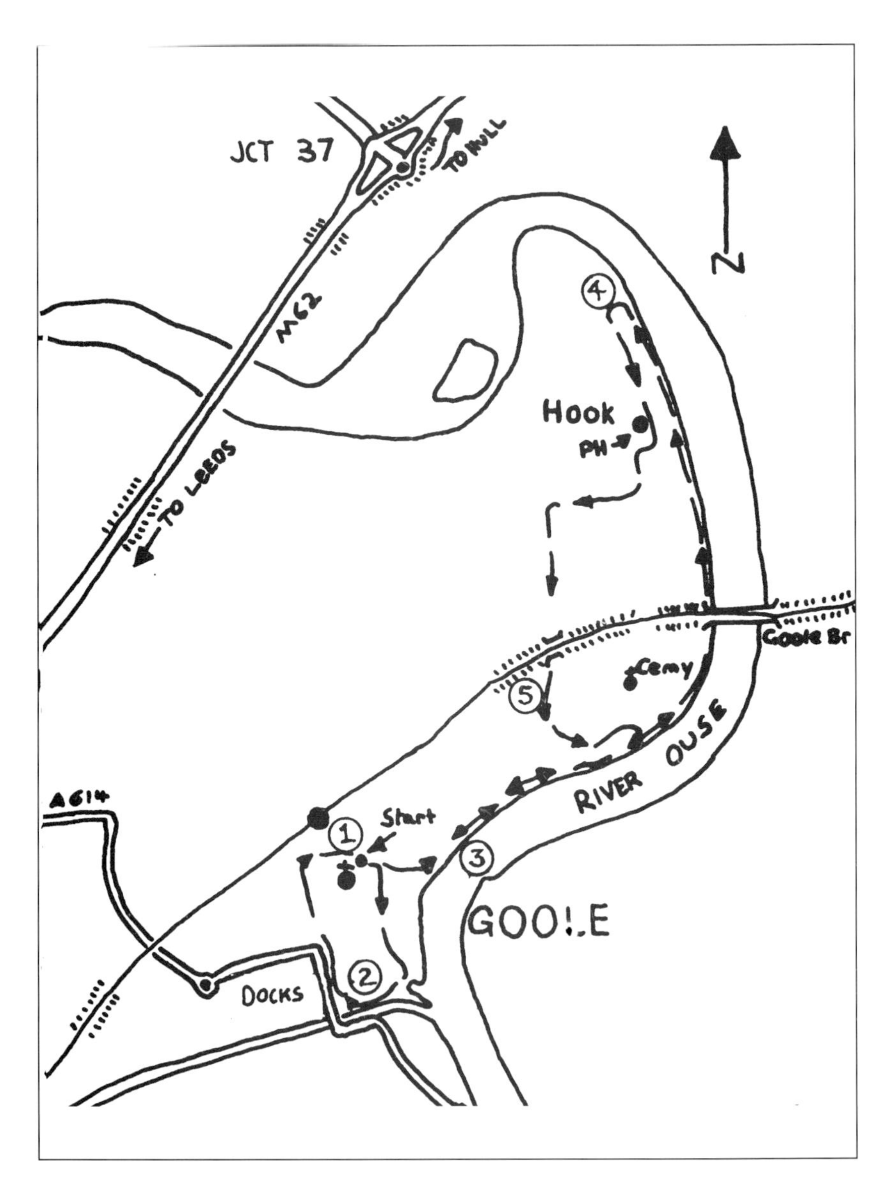

After crossing a second bridge, turn right on Stanhope Street passing the old L & Y R Goods Office and, on the corner, the red brick and terracotta Bank Chambers of 1892. Pass the Old George and continue along Boothferry Road and North Street to reach the Ouse Bank.

3. Turn left along the bank footpath, passing the linear park, and walk on alongside the houses.

A monster sturgeon was fished out of this reach of the Ouse in 1904. It weighed 16 stones and was 8 feet 10 inches long.

Continue on the path, passing the cemetery, and swing left under the Goole Railway Bridge to Hook.

Girded by a pronounced Ouse loop, shy and secret Hook takes its name from Baron John de Houke who came over with William the Conqueror. At the site of an important ferry crossing to Howdendyke it once had an impressive manor house but only a moat remains. There are two distinctive buildings in the village - the 13th-century church of St Mary and Hook Hall, a red-brick Georgian mansion erected in 1743 for Admiral Frank Sotheron, a mate of Nelson.

Cross a stile by an unusual round house, go through two gates and cross two further stiles, swinging left off the embankment to a new estate road - Ferry Lane.

4. Walk on and turn left along High Street. The entrance to Hook Hall is on the right. Pass the Sotheron Arms and go right on Church Lane for about 150 yards and turn left along a public footpath. Weave right by the school and turn right, following a public footpath sign on a track along a ditch. Cross a bridge in the field corner and turn left on a cinder track, continuing under the railway bridge.

5. Veer right, following a hedgeline, and continue alongside the gardens, swinging left into an estate. Turn right on Montrose Drive and go left on Wentworth Drive. Turn right and go left into the recreation park, regaining the Ouse bank. Continue back to the starting place.

Places of Interest Nearby

Goole Museum and Art Gallery, where you can see displays charting the development of Goole and the Aire and Calder Canal Company (telephone: 01405 722251). Also in Goole is the *Waterways Museum and Adventure Centre* (telephone: 01405 768730).

WALK 20

HUMBER BRIDGE AND BANKS: A SENSATIONAL SORTIE

This walk takes us across the bridge to the riverside Visitor Centre and back; a longer alternative route leads on to the fascinating town of Barton-on-Humber. From artisan terrace housing and warehouses to mansions, schools, municipal buildings, chapels and churches, the architectural history of Barton beams out, acknowledged in a succession of brightly painted civic plaques. Such an array of architectural styles. Such a refreshing pride!

The mighty bridge over the Humber.

Without a boarding card, this is the nearest walkers get to flying. Swooping over the Humber in a spectacular leap of 4,626 feet, the Humber Bridge was opened to traffic in June 1981. Since then, its debt charges have accelerated faster than the tolls from the cars and juggernauts that thunder across it. Not that walkers need care. If you are wind-braced, vertigo free and untroubled by the occasional oscillations – referred to by the engineers as 'longitudinal movement and vertical and lateral rotation' – then you can stride across for free. And once you get to the far bank, there are more objects of interest than you can throw a brick at, the process of tile and brickmaking having left a legacy of old clay pits that are fast becoming one of the premier habitats for wildlife in northern England.

Before Barton's skyline was dominated by the new bridge, its most visually prominent buildings were its twin churches and the six-sailed Old Mill on Market Lane. This was built in 1803 on the site of an early Norman castle. Originally it was used for chalk grinding but in 1815 it was enlarged for processing barley and malt. Gas driven after the removal of its sails in 1868, the mill continued working until 1950. Since that time it has been imaginatively restored, preserving many of its beams, cogs and gearing to create a unique pub and restaurant.

If you choose to do the longer walk you can visit the Old Mill before exploring the area of clay pits west of Barton. You will find a varied standard menu supplemented by daily specials. From the extensive printed list, diners can choose from a range of dishes including beef and ale pie, gammon steak, chicken kiev, salmon and hot stuffed baguettes. The blackboard choices are typically turkey and ham pie, spinach and ricotta canneloni, chicken madras and lamb chops. A Marston's inn, the Old Mill serves Marston's Bitter and Pedigree together with Carlsberg, Foster's and Stella Artois lagers. Opening times are 11.30 am to 3 pm and 6 pm to 11 pm from Monday to Saturday. Sunday hours are 12 noon to 3 pm and 7 pm to 10.30 pm. Telephone: 01652 660333.

- **HOW TO GET THERE:** In the shadow of the bridge, the start of the walk is signposted off the A63, 'Humber Bridge Country Park' and 'Hessle Viewing Area'.
- **PARKING:** Extensive free parking is available adjacent to the Country Park (follow signs). The parking areas are open from 5 am to 8 pm daily. From May to September, the opening time is extended by 30 minutes.
- **LENGTH OF THE WALK:** 4½ miles (café refreshments available in the car park) or 8½ miles. Map: OS Landranger 107 Kingston upon Hull and surrounding area (starting point GR 022256).

THE WALK

1. Walk across the car park towards the bridge and swing left under the bridge following the signposted pedestrian path to Barton, turning left up the steps and left again along the walkway.

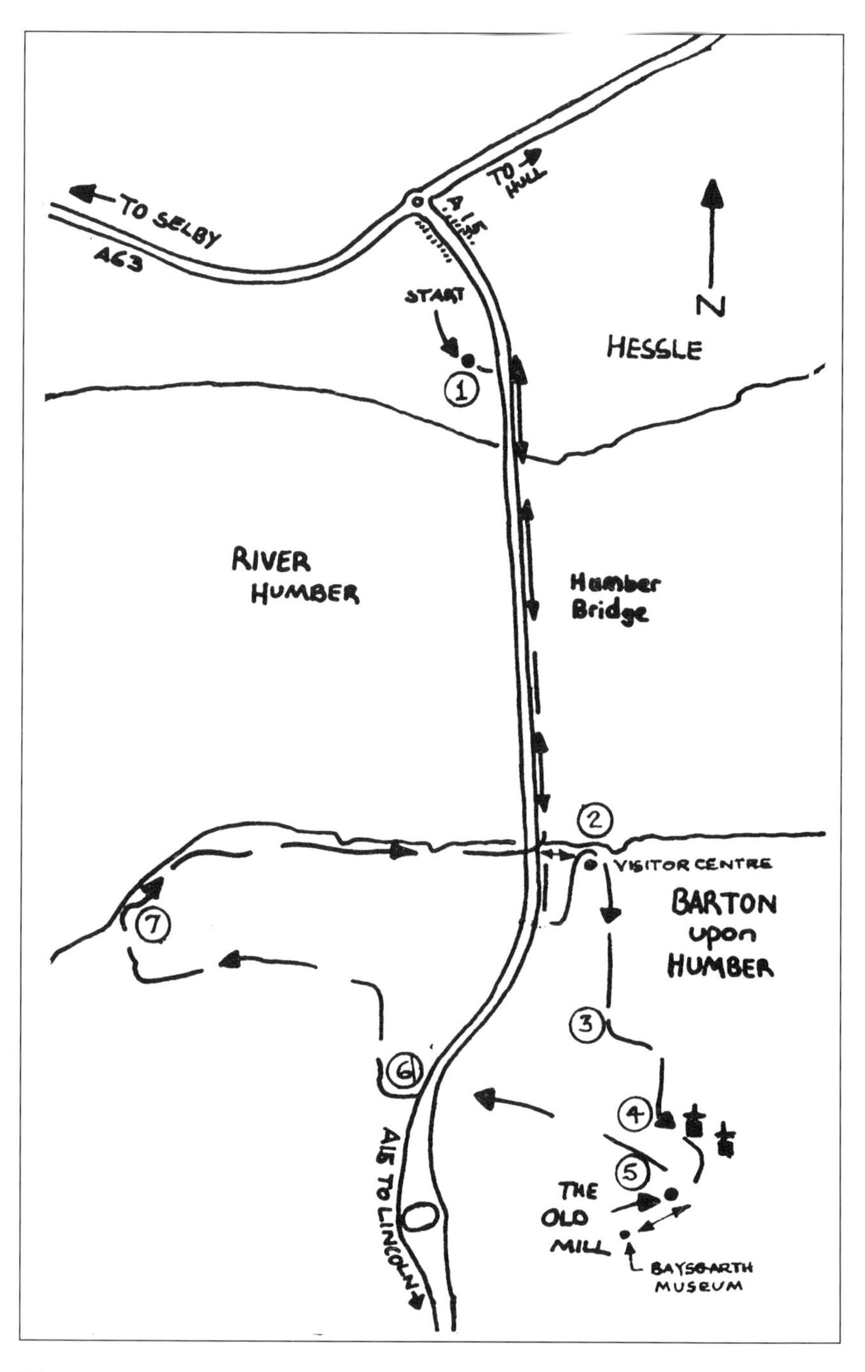
TO SELBY
A63
TO HULL
A15
START
1
N
HESSLE
RIVER
HUMBER
Humber
Bridge
2
VISITOR CENTRE
BARTON
upon
HUMBER
7
3
6
4
5
A15 TO LINCOLN
THE
OLD
MILL
BAYSGARTH
MUSEUM

The Old Mill in Market Lane.

Ever since man first set out upon the Humber in his dug out log-boats he has dreamed of a bridge. It took 44,000 miles of wire, 27,000 tonnes of steel, and 480,000 tonnes of concrete to build. Today, vehicles can speed across the river in little over a minute, cutting some road distances by 50 miles and saving countless hours.

Continue along the bridge to the far bank and pass the Barton sign, going left down the steps and left again to the road. At the junction, cross the road to the footpath and turn right. Just before the terrace housing go left on a footpath hedgeside, passing the ponds and reedbeds. Walk on to the Humber bank and turn right to the Visitor Centre.

This former coastguard station of 1880 marks the start of the 140 miles-long Viking Way between Barton and Okeham.

2. For the shorter walk, retrace your steps back to the start from here. For the longer walk, turn right past Barton Haven and follow the creek up along Waterside road.

Note the interesting warehouse of 1807. Just beyond, is that the longest continuous red-tiled roof in the world?

3. Continue past the railway station and turn left along Butts Road.

Proudly in line, eight very distinctive villas grace this road.

Turn right along Queen's Avenue and continue straight ahead along Queen's Street.

On the right is a school of 1831. Its first master was Sir Isaac Pitman, the inventor of Pitman's shorthand.

4. Go left on High Street and Burgate to St Mary's.

St Chad came to Barton in AD 669 to found this famous church.

Continue to the roundabout and go left, walking on the cobbled street between St Peter's Lodge and Beck Hill. Continue on the footpath and go left into the grounds of St Peter's church.

Dating from the 10th century, this exquisite redundant church is in the care of English Heritage. Near the church boundary is Barton's oldest house - Tyrwhitt Hall - the former home of musician Phillip Pape, the creator of the Barton Symphony Orchestra in the 1940s.

Go back to the roundabout and turn left on Whitecross Street, continuing on this street across the next junction to the Baysgarth Rural Crafts Museum (free entry).

This excellent museum tells the story of the local industries, including tile and brickmaking. Open Thursdays, Fridays and bank holidays from 10.30 am to 3.30 pm and at weekends from 10.30 am to 4.30 pm.

Walk back down Whitecross Street and go left to the Old Mill.

5. Continue along Market Lane and Hollydyke past the fire station and at the roundabout keep going straight forward, following the signs to the Humber Bridge Viewing Area. At the next bend continue forward on the cul-de-sac Westfield Road.

6. At the end of the road go under the Humber Bridge approach, using the pedestrian underpass. Climb the steps and keep going forward for about 300 yards. Turn right, following the public footpath sign along the hedge, continuing to the field corner. Go left for 80 yards and go right over the dyke bridge turning left along the lane to the T junction. Keep going forward, cross a stile and follow the public footpath towards a copse.

As you approach the trees you may hear the hypnotic plop and gurgle of a fulsome spring. At some time in the past it has been brick-lined but it now seems abandoned.

Cross the dyke on the planked bridge and swing left and right over the tussocky field, walking on hedgeside to the corner. Go right on the farm track following the byway sign. Continue to the banks of the river.

7. Turn right, passing the Far Ings Nature Reserve. Walkers have free access to the five birdwatching hides. Continue along the Humber path (a short track on the left leads to the ruined wharves and manufacturing buildings) past the hotel and the working tileyard to the Visitor Centre. Retrace your steps from here back to the starting point.

Places of Interest Nearby

There is much to see and do in Hull, including the *Town Docks Museum* which charts the history of the fishing industry, *'Streetlife' Transport Museum* and *Wilberforce House* which has displays about the slave trade and emancipation. (For more details of all three, telephone: 01482 613902). The *Marina* is fascinating and there are two historic and atmospheric old inns: the *Black Boy* on High Street (telephone: 01482 326516) and the *White Harte* on Silver Street/Bowlalley Lane (telephone: 01482 326363).